MULTICULTURAL EDUCATION SERIES

James A. Banks, Series Editor

continued

DIVERSITY AND THE NEW TEACHER

Learning from Experience in Urban Schools

Catherine Cornbleth

Teachers College
Columbia University
New York and London

KH

Published by Teachers College Press, 1234 Amsterdam Avenue, New York, NY 10027

Library of Congress Cataloging-in-Publication Data

Cornbleth, Catherine.
  Diversity and the new teacher : learning from experience in urban schools / Catherine Cornbleth.
      p. cm. — (Multicultural education series)
  Includes bibliographical references and index.
  ISBN-13: 978-0-8077-4896-1 (pbk. : alk. paper)
  ISBN-13: 978-0-8077-4897-8 (hardcover : alk. paper)
    1. Education, Urban—United States—Case studies.   2. Multicultural education—United States—Case studies.   3. First year teachers—United States—Case studies.   I. Title.
  LC5131.C635 2008
  370.9173'2—dc22

                                                                              2008010123

ISBN 978-0-8077-4896-1 (paper)
ISBN 978-0-8077-4897-8 (hardcover)

Printed on acid-free paper
Manufactured in the United States of America

15 14 13 12 11 10 09 08   8 7 6 5 4 3 2 1

9/3/09

Contents

Series Foreword

The nation's deepening ethnic texture, interracial tension and conflict, and the increasing percentage of students who speak a first language other than English make multicultural education imperative. The U.S. Census (2007) estimates that people of color made up 28% of the nation's population in 2000 and predicts that they will make up 38% in 2025 and 50% in 2050.

American classrooms are experiencing the largest influx of immigrant students since the beginning of the 20th century. About a million immigrants are making the United States their home each year (Martin & Midgley, 1999). Almost four million (3,780,019) legal immigrants settled in the United States between 2000 and 2004. Only 15% came from nations in Europe. Most (66%) came from nations in Asia, from Mexico, and from nations in Latin America, Central America, and the Caribbean (U.S. Department of Homeland Security, 2004). A large but undetermined number of undocumented immigrants also enter the United States each year. In 2007, *The New York Times* estimated that there were 12 million illegal immigrants in the United States (Immigration Sabotage, 2007). The influence of an increasingly ethnically diverse population on U.S. schools, colleges, and universities is and will continue to be enormous.

Schools in the United States are characterized by rich ethnic, cultural, language, and religious diversity. U.S. schools are more diverse today than they have been since the early 1900s when a flood of immigrants entered the United States from Southern, Central, and Eastern Europe. In the thirty-year period between 1973 and 2004, the percentage of students of color in U.S. public schools increased from 22% to 43%. If current trends continue, students of color might equal or exceed the percentage of White students in U.S. public schools within one or two decades. Students of color already exceed the number of Whites students in six states: California, Hawaii, Louisiana, Mississippi, New Mexico, and Texas (Dillon, 2006).

Language and religious diversity is also increasing among the U.S. student population. In 2000, about 20% of the school-age population spoke a language at home other than English (U.S. Census Bureau, 2007). Harvard professor Diana L. Eck (2001) calls the United States the "most religiously diverse nation on earth" (p. 4). Islam is now the fastest-growing religion in the United States, as well as in several European nations such as France and the United Kingdom (Cesari, 2004). Most teachers now in the classroom and in teacher education programs are likely to have students from diverse ethnic, racial, language, and religious groups in their classrooms during their careers. This is true for both inner-city and suburban teachers.

An important goal of multicultural education is to improve race relations and to help all students acquire the knowledge, attitudes, and skills needed to participate in cross-cultural interactions and in personal, social, and civic action that will help make our nation more democratic and just. Multicultural education is consequently as important for middle-class White suburban students as it is for students of color who live in the inner city. Multicultural education fosters the public good and the overarching goals of the commonwealth.

The major purpose of the *Multicultural Education Series* is to provide preservice educators, practicing educators, graduate students, scholars, and policymakers with an interrelated and comprehensive set of books that summarizes and analyzes important research, theory, and practice related to the education of ethnic, racial, cultural, and language groups in the United States and the education of mainstream students about diversity. The books in the *Series* provide research, theoretical, and practical knowledge about the behaviors and learning characteristics of students of color, language-minority students, and low-income students. They also provide knowledge about ways to improve academic achievement and race relations in educational settings.

The definition of multicultural education in the *Handbook of Research on Multicultural Education* (Banks & Banks, 2004) is used in the *Series*: Multicultural education is "a field of study designed to increase educational equity for all students that incorporates, for this purpose, content, concepts, principles, theories, and paradigms from history, the social and behavioral sciences, and particularly from ethnic studies and women's studies" (p. xii). In the *Series*, as in the *Handbook*, multicultural education is considered a "metadiscipline."

The dimensions of multicultural education, developed by Banks (2004) and described in the *Handbook of Research on Multicultural Education*, provide the conceptual framework for the development of the publications in the *Series*. They are: *content integration, the knowledge construction process, prejudice reduction, an equity pedagogy,* and *an empowering school culture and social structure*. To implement multicultural education effectively, teachers and administrators must attend to each of the five dimensions of multicultural education. They should use content from diverse groups when teaching concepts and skills, help students to understand how knowledge in the various disciplines is constructed, help students to develop positive intergroup attitudes and behaviors, and modify their teaching strategies so that students from different racial, cultural, language, and social-class groups will experience equal educational opportunities. The total environment and culture of the school must also be transformed so that students from diverse groups will experience equal status in the culture and life of the school.

Although the five dimensions of multicultural education are highly interrelated, each requires deliberate attention and focus. Each publication in the *Series* focuses on one or more of the dimensions, although each book deals with all of them to some extent because of the highly interrelated characteristics of the dimensions.

Helping teachers to gain the knowledge, skills, and attitudes to work with students from diverse racial, cultural, ethnic, and language groups is one of the most difficult and complex tasks in the profession. In this engaging, edifying, and heartfelt book, Cornbleth blends her deep knowledge of schools and race with her pedagogical experiences and insights to craft a book that is a significant contribution to both the theory and practice of teaching. It is replete with wisdom, insights, and suggestions that both new and experience teachers—as well as theorists and researchers—will find helpful and informative.

Cornbleth constructs a typology of teachers in the process of becoming that reveals the complex and nuanced process of how and why teachers experience varying levels of success in diverse classrooms and schools. The typology is a significant theoretical and practical contribution to the teacher education literature. Cornbleth defines each category of the typology, gives richly textured and thick descriptions of teacher education students who exemplify them, and deftly describes which attributes should be encouraged and nurtured in teacher education programs. She also describes the challenges, dilemmas, possibilities, and journeys that students in the process of becoming teachers experience as they struggle to construct their self-definitions as teachers.

Teachers who exemplify *radical individualism* "reject or attempt to ignore group-linked differences." Cornbleth describes how this approach includes colorblindness or colormute (Pollock, 2004) stances toward dealing with student difference. Teachers who view their students as "others" who are distinct from them and require control exemplify a *worlds apart* conception. The more successful teachers studied by Cornbleth embraced the *bridging different worlds* conception. These teachers work diligently to connect with their students, to understand and make use of their experiences, and to communicate with them effectively. Cornbleth uses vivid and revealing case studies and vignettes to describe the challenges and opportunities of becoming an effective teacher in diverse classrooms and schools. If heeded, the messages in this timely, informative, and practical book can help teachers in diverse schools and classrooms become not only more skillful and reflective professionals, but also more caring human beings.

James A. Banks

REFERENCES

Banks, J. A. (2004). Multicultural education: Historical development, dimensions, and practice. In J. A. Banks & C. A. M. Banks (Eds.), *Handbook of research on multicultural education* (2nd ed., pp. 3–29). San Francisco: Jossey-Bass.

Banks, J. A., & Banks, C. A. M. (Eds.). (2004). *Handbook of research on multicultural education* (2nd ed.). San Francisco: Jossey-Bass.

Cesari, J. (2004). *When Islam and democracy meet: Muslims in Europe and the United States.* New York: Pelgrave Macmillan.

Dillon, S. (2006, August 27). In schools across U.S., the melting pot overflows. *New York Times*, pp. A7, A16.

Eck, D. L. (2001). *A new religious America: How a "Christian country" has become the world's most religiously diverse nation.* New York: HarperSanFrancisco.

Immigration sabotage [Editorial]. (2007, June 4). *New York Times*, p. A22.

Martin, P., & Midgley, E. (1999). Immigration to the United States. *Population Bulletin, 54*(2), 1–44. Washington, DC: Population Reference Bureau.

Pollock, M. (2004). *Colormute: Race talk in an American school.* Princeton, NJ: Princeton University Press.

United States Census Bureau. (2007). *Statistical abstract of the United States* (126th ed.). Washington, DC: U.S. Government Printing Office.

United States Department of Homeland Security. (2004). *Yearbook of immigration statistics, 2004.* Washington, DC: Office of Immigration Statistics, Author. Retrieved September 6, 2006, from www.uscis.gov/graphics/shared/statistics/yearbook/Yearbook2004.pdf

Acknowledgments

The "we" who worked on the project that provides most of the cases and vignettes in *Diversity and the New Teacher* are three graduate students and myself. During the first year, Elizabeth Holmes and Bridget Caffrey, both white and from another part of the state (Bridget) and Canada (Liz), did most of the fieldwork at Charter School while I was at Royalton. During the second year, Ursuline Bankhead, African American and from the city in which the project was conducted, worked with me at Royalton. Without their conscientious, perceptive assistance and patience with my unending questions, the project would not have been possible. As of this writing, Liz and Ursie have completed their doctorates in counseling psychology and taken positions in Toronto and Buffalo, respectively. Bridget has completed a reading specialist master's degree and is teaching in New York.

My appreciation for their support and constructive feedback in the shaping, writing, and/or refining of *Diversity and the New Teacher* goes to several key people, including David Cantaffa, Marlene Smithers, Lois Weis, and Carolyn Wolck. For enabling the research project, I appreciate the support of the university teacher education program staff and education school dean, Royalton High School and Charter School administrators, faculty, and staff. Dean Mary Gresham also provided invaluable graduate student and interview transcription support for the project.

Many thanks to Multicultural Education series editor Jim Banks for inviting me on this journey, and to Brian Ellerbeck, executive editor at Teachers College Press, who played a major role in shaping this volume in ways I had not even imagined in the beginning.

Special appreciation goes to the new teachers who allowed me into their lives and experiences at Royalton and Charter School. You have made major contributions to the education of countless future teachers and their students.

Catherine Cornbleth

1

Challenges Here, Now, and Ahead

Hillary Swank as English teacher Erin Gruwell at Wilson High School in Long Beach, California, in the 2007 film *Freedom Writers*. Morgan Freeman as bullhorn– and baseball bat–carrying principal Joe Clark of Eastside High School in Paterson, New Jersey, in the 1989 film *Lean on Me*. Edward James Olmos as math teacher Jaime Escalante at Garfield High School in East Los Angeles in the 1988 film *Stand and Deliver*. All three popular films portray rowdy to chaotic, sometimes violent, urban high schools with inadequate resources and mostly white teachers who have given up on their predominantly working-class and poor African American and/or Hispanic students. A few teachers and administrators are openly racist and do not disguise their low expectations for "those students."

Enter teacher or principal superhero who almost single-handedly turns around a class or an entire school. Together, the superheroes and their students prove the naysayers wrong, and the movies end before the beginning of the next school year.

All three films are "based on a true story" and, with other films, books, and media portrayals, shape public perceptions of urban schools and students. While we know that the primary purpose of such films is to make money, we too often forget that this usually means telling "a good story" with action, drama, and a leading actor with box office draw. That means some distortion (sometimes quite a bit) of life in urban high schools. At least since the days of George Washington and Davy Crockett, Americans have favored heroes of mythic proportions. A math teacher who gets barrio kids to take his calculus class and gets all 18 to pass the Advanced Placement (AP) calculus exam is our kind of hero. So should be the students who surmount substantial obstacles in their daily lives to pass the exam twice (because Educational Testing Service, which administers the exam, did not believe their scores were accurate the first time).

Unfortunately, such "good stories" exaggerate extreme cases, good or bad, and unfairly portray many, if not most, urban students, teachers, and schools. They certainly do little to encourage new teachers to teach in "the city." Most of us are not superhuman. We do not want to give up our personal and family lives or pay the price of divorce or heart attack as do the heroes of these films. We live in the "real world" where students, teachers, and schools are neither all good nor all bad.

In this book, you will meet "real" prospective and newer teachers and their urban students and schools, ones you will never see on the cineplex screen despite their noteworthy successes and failures. The successful new teachers work hard, learn from their mistakes, reach out to their students, and maintain positive expectations for meaningful academic teaching and learning. They are good teachers in-the-making.

The student bodies at the two schools featured here are diverse: primarily African American, Hispanic, and white with some Asian, Native American, and refugee students from various world regions. They are not affluent. The high school building is old, well maintained but lacking adequate teaching-learning facilities and materials. The elementary school building is newly remodeled, superbly maintained, and boasts ample materials and expanding facilities. There are fights at the high school, sometimes nasty, but rarely if ever *between* racial/ethnic groups or threatening to nonparticipants. In both schools, African American, Hispanic, white students, and others seem to get along. Too many, however, are not well prepared educationally, academically inclined, or cooperative "good students."

The primary purpose of *Diversity and the New Teacher* is to assist new teachers in getting started, surviving, and succeeding in urban schools with diverse student populations by sharing the actual experiences of new teachers during field experience, student-teaching, or the first years of teaching. Aside from a few fine personal accounts such as Greg Michie's *Holler if You Hear Me* (1999), there is very little literature about new teachers' experiences with diverse groups of students, most of whom are different from themselves. There is a fair bit of advice, but it is rarely linked to the actual experiences of new teachers or portrayed in the new teachers' own voices as is done here.

This gap in our knowledge about new teachers' experiences and learning in urban schools is what prompted "the project" that grounds this book (see Appendix A for specifics about the field research). Via observations, interviews, and informal conversations, I followed three cohorts of prospective teachers through their fall semester Field Experience and spring semester Student-Teaching, two at Royalton High School and one at Charter School, grades 1–5. These new teachers are the main characters in the chapters that follow, with a supporting cast drawn from the available literature.

Importantly, most of the new teachers in the project (14 of 16) are white, as are the large majority of teachers in U.S. public schools. Most of their students are not, which is typical in urban centers and some metropolitan areas. Consequently, the focus here is on new white teachers working with students who are different from themselves, not only racially/ethnically different, but also different in terms of socioeconomic status, first language, religion, or academic ability/motivation. A second key feature is that the students in these schools and classes are not only different from their teachers; they also differ from one another in one or more of the ways just listed. In other words, the student populations are diverse. Clearly, the current generation of new teachers faces major changes in the backgrounds, popular cultures, and expectations of the students in U.S. public schools, K–12. *Diversity and the New Teacher* is intended to assist new teachers in facing those changes more successfully.

It is difficult to remain unaware of the changing demographics of the United States or its public school student population—more students of color and more cultural diversity among students—or that, as a group, U.S. public school teachers remain overwhelmingly white and middle-class. Changes in the student population mean, among other things, that the old or traditional ways of teaching are no longer appropriate or effective for many students. What was good enough for us or our parents is not good enough for today's students any more than is the technology of the 1970s.

Also difficult to ignore are substantive achievement gaps between white students and most students of color (for a fuller view of demographic data and trends, see, e.g., Villegas & Lucas, 2002; Cochran-Smith, Davis, & Fries, 2004). The gaps may be narrowing for some groups, grade levels, and subjects, but they remain unacceptable. As in the economy, the rich are getting richer, while the poor are becoming relatively poorer. Moreover, public schools are increasingly resegregated, and the schools deemed to be failing are rarely those of middle- and upper-middle-class white students (see, e.g., Tatum, 2007; Harvard Civil Rights Project, www .civilrightsproject.harvard.edu; National Center for Educational Statistics, www.nces.gov).

Attention to difference and diversity is not an optional add-on or decoration to display "political correctness" or help people feel good about themselves or others. Increasingly, difference and diversity are a way of life in our globalizing society. It is difficult, if not impossible, to isolate oneself from "others," and it would be counterproductive for all concerned to try to do so. Yet many prospective teachers still have little or no knowledge of or experience with people who are different from themselves. Upward of 80% of teachers are white and middle-class. Most of their future students in public schools are neither. The track record of teacher education in preparing teachers to deal constructively with difference and diversity has not been encouraging (e.g., Zeichner, 1992; Zeichner & Hoeft,

1996; Ladson-Billings, 1999b). The few exceptions (e.g., Ladson-Billings, 2001) are just that.

In this volume, constructive engagement with diversity is assumed to be shaped by the school setting, including its culture or ethos, what prospective and newer teachers bring to the school, and their experiences at the school site. Quality teaching and teacher education, like fairness, are context-sensitive.

I focus on field experience and student teaching in urban schools because it is here that most prospective teachers (1) encounter difference face-to-face in schools that are different from their own and with students who are different from themselves, and (2) actually perform the profession for which they have been preparing. They are not reading about English Language Learners (ELLs), for example, or teaching a lesson on critical reading to their peers in an on-campus class. They are in schools, with students, and are expected "to teach."

Field experiences, including student-teaching, are professional learning settings as well as practice sites. In various ways, they "teach" prospective and new teachers how to do their job, and may have as much or more influence as college courses and professional development workshops. Yet teacher educators know relatively little in any systematic and specific way about what happens, for example, to student-teachers or interns in the schools where we "place" them. Consequently, *Diversity and the New Teacher* also is intended to narrow that gap and inform teacher educators so we can better prepare new teachers. In other words, what might teacher educators and prospective teachers learn from the interaction of individual and institution in school settings during pre-student-teaching field experiences and student teaching itself that could better prepare new teachers for constructively engaging student difference and diversity? Responding to that question is my major reason for writing this book. Prospective and newer teachers reading *Diversity and the New Teacher* may well glimpse themselves in these pages and find both impetus and guidance for strengthening academic relationships with the range of students they face in their own classes each day.

In the sections that follow, I note my interpretations of difference and diversity, briefly review the relevant research and professional literature, and then describe the teacher education program and two urban schools that provide the context for the experiences to be highlighted and the stories to be told in subsequent chapters. The prospective teachers (PTs) who are the main characters in these pages are introduced. (The methodology of the project and the theoretical perspective framing this volume are described in Appendix A. The PTs are listed in Appendix B.) Lastly, I provide an overview of the following chapters.

A NOTE ON DIFFERENCE AND DIVERSITY

I use difference, as indicated above, to refer to student-teacher difference, especially differences between students and preservice or newer teachers such as race/ethnicity, socioeconomic status, first or home language, religion, and academic ability/motivation. For example, 14 of 16 prospective teachers I followed through Field Experience and Student-Teaching are white, about three-quarters are from middle-class or more affluent families, English is their first language, they are at least nominally Christian, and they are good to excellent students. Most of their students are African American or Hispanic; few come from middle-class homes, and a majority has yet to demonstrate academic ability or motivation to do well in school. Some are not Christian (Islam appears to be the second most common religion at the two focus schools), and others are not native speakers of English.

By student diversity, I refer to schools and classes with students who are different from one another with respect to race/ethnicity, socioeconomic status, home language, religion, or academic ability/motivation. In this view, a single student cannot be diverse. If s/he is of mixed ancestry, s/he is of mixed ancestry, but not diverse in the sense used here. Sometimes, I hear teachers refer to multicultural or diverse authors when they mean an African American or Hispanic author. I do not condone that usage. Similarly, a class of African American (or Hispanic or any other racialized or ethnic group) is not diverse; it is African American or Hispanic.

Of course, I recognize that in one way or another, every teacher is different from every student in some way, especially if age and education are considered. That technically correct observation, however, deflects attention from the racial/ethnic, social class, and other critical ruptures in U.S. society that advantage some groups and individuals at the expense of others, thus serving to sustain those advantages. Instead, teachers ought to face the differences and divides and attempt to deal with them in equitable and constructive ways—as will be illustrated in later chapters. Difference by itself is not a problem—unless we make it a problem. If there is a problem, it is ours, not our students', even though they will suffer any negative consequences.

The reciprocity of difference also deserves mention. That is, students and teachers are different from one another in the settings of interest here. It is not only the case that students are different than their teachers; the reverse is also true. The stories to be told depend on the speaker or starting point. *Diversity and the New Teacher* need not take the teachers' perspective as it does here. It also could have been told from the students' perspectives.

WHERE WE'VE BEEN AND WHAT WE KNOW ABOUT
CONSTRUCTIVE ENGAGEMENT WITH DIFFERENCE AND DIVERSITY

Three substantive reviews by well-respected colleagues in teacher educa-tion (Zeichner, 1992 [also, see Zeichner & Hoeft, 1996]; Ladson-Billings, 1999b; Sleeter, 2001) and my search through more recent literature are in-formative, if not encouraging. Studies of the effects of so-called multicultural college classes, with or without field experiences in the "real world," on prospective teachers' beliefs and attitudes can point the way toward bet-ter teacher preparation for those real worlds but do not examine what ac-tually happens in classroom practice (Sleeter, 2001). Although new teachers usually report that student-teaching is the most influential or helpful part of their teacher education experience (e.g., Hollins, 1995), the evidence regarding its effects is equivocal (see, e.g., Zeichner & Gore, 1990). It is well documented in sociology and social psychology that setting influences behavior. Yet there is relatively little systematically obtained evidence about what happens during field experience, student-teaching, and initial teach-ing experiences, especially with respect to engaging student difference and diversity. In fact, more than token attention of any kind to difference and diversity in teacher education is a relatively recent phenomenon (Zeichner, 1992). This may be the result of "cultural encapsulation" wherein primarily white, middle-class prospective teachers are prepared by predominantly white faculties (who themselves were also prepared by predominantly white faculties) for successful teaching in relatively homogeneous white, middle-class schools (Zeichner, 1992). Relatively few of these prospective teach-ers have come from or say that they would like to teach in urban areas.

In a 1999 book chapter, "Preparing Teachers for Diversity," Gloria Ladson-Billings (1999b) provides historical perspective and a review of research published during the 1980s and early 1990s. Particularly relevant to *Diversity and the New Teacher*, Ladson-Billings reminds readers that there was negligible change in teacher education to deal constructively with earlier immigrants or desegregated schools. Neither of the major teacher education reform reports of the 1980s (Holmes Group, 1986; Carnegie Forum's Task Force, 1986) addressed the preparation of teachers for an increasingly diverse student population. Widely heard calls for a break in this 20th-century history of maintaining the white, middle-class status quo did not come until the 1990s.

Only gradually have some teacher education programs begun to in-clude courses or redesign courses and field experiences intended to pre-pare teachers to work well with students who are different from themselves. No wonder one finds so little research about effectively teaching diverse groups of students in the mainstream scholarly literature. Ladson-Billings's literature search identified only 25 data-based, published articles relevant to teacher preparation for working with culturally diverse students during the 13-year period 1981–1993, half of which were course or program descriptions. Most of the remaining pieces measured prospective teachers' multicultural knowledge (e.g., African American history), attitudes, and/or skills before and/or after a multicultural course or the teacher education program as a whole. Neither single courses nor an intensive 3-day workshop were shown to change prospective teachers' attitudes toward students different from themselves, perhaps because of the much greater weight of prior experience and other coursework. Similarly, in an extensive review of research on learning to teach, Wideen, Mayer-Smith, and Moon (1998) found that the three studies examining the impact of incorporating multicultural approaches into traditional programs of teacher education demonstrated "raised awareness," but the programs "have done little to alter the prior beliefs of the beginning teachers" (p. 146). Adding multicultural or culturally relevant subject matter to the traditional teacher education curriculum appears to be insufficient for changing attitudes without accompanying efforts to assist prospective teachers in examining their assumptions, perceptions, and expectations of students of color.

A different approach, taken by Sleeter (1988), surveyed Wisconsin teachers with multicultural preparation and found that elementary teachers were more likely than secondary teachers to report using multicultural materials and content, as were literature and art teachers compared with math and science teachers. Importantly, teachers more often reported using materials and information about women than about racial and ethnic groups.

There is evidence suggesting that more extended experience in communities different from one's own and courses that go beyond multicultural content to examine structural or institutional racism and white privilege can make a positive difference. Unfortunately, antiracist and other "against the grain" perspectives also have been shown to prompt resistance from white prospective teachers who have come to take their unseen white privilege for granted (e.g., Rothenberg, 1988) and who challenge both the message and the messenger of antiracism. Some noteworthy recent efforts to confront white privilege and passive racism in teacher education programs have moved cautiously after establishing positive instructor-student relationships to minimize prospective teachers' defensiveness and resistance (e.g., McIntyre, 1997; Marx, 2006). In studying four sections of a multicultural course, Brown (2004) found that efforts to "reduce resistance and nurture and reinforce the message has a greater influence" than the message alone (p. 325).

Ladson-Billings (1999b) invokes King's (1991) conception of "dysconscious racism" to understand whites' resistance to changing their beliefs about difference and diversity. According to King (1991, p. 135), *dysconscious racism* is "an uncritical habit of mind (including perceptions, attitudes, assumptions, and beliefs) that justifies inequity and exploitation by accepting the existing order of things as given," including mainstream white norms and privilege. Moreover, prospective teachers, as will be illustrated in later chapters, may see diversity as a problem rather than a resource because they assume that it leads to divisiveness, tensions, and hostilities. Consequently, they may want students to be or behave more like themselves. Ironically, however, for African American, Latina/o, and other students of color, a strong racial or ethnocultural identity is associated with academic success (e.g., Tharp, 1989; Davidson, Yu, & Phelan, 1993).

Zeichner's (1992; see also Zeichner & Hoeft, 1996) review includes a broader range of literature and looks to "consensus" in the field of teacher education where data are scarce. Here, I focus on the research, which Zeichner concludes has "clearly demonstrated the very limited long-term impact of the segregated approach [adding on a unit or course about diversity, in contrast to integration or infusion throughout the program] on the attitudes, beliefs, and teaching practices of teacher education students" (1992, p. 13). In fact, readings or didactic presentations about groups (e.g., Hispanics, poor families) can encourage overgeneralization and reinforce stereotypes.

With respect to field experience and student-teaching, Zeichner points to agreement on the desirability of placements in schools serving diverse groups of students and the importance of continuing support and guided reflection to help prospective teachers interpret their experiences in ways that do not simply reinforce stereotypes. Wideen, Mayer-Smith, and Moon (1998) noted that in 25 studies of student-teaching they reviewed, the influence of students in classrooms "on the student teaching experience remains virtually unexplored" (p. 153). Further, placements in primarily black or diverse schools were not necessarily associated with more student-teachers reporting positive attitudes or knowledge about the student groups that differed from themselves.

Sleeter's (2001) more recent research review finds few studies that have moved beyond looking for course-related knowledge gains or attitude changes of white prospective teachers to examine what they do in actual classroom practice. From the research, she adds to the picture of white prospective teachers sketched above that most have little awareness or understanding of discrimination and especially of structural inequalities and racism, that many doubt their ability to teach African American students, and that most have little, if any, cross-cultural experience. Moreover, there is evidence that white prospective teachers "tend to use colorblindness as a way of coping with fear and ignorance" (2001, p. 95). Only one study was identified that examined carryover from multicultural course-work into student-teaching. Lawrence (1997) found wide variation in carry-over positively related to prospective teachers' level of racial awareness.

Sleeter concluded that, of the various teacher education strategies that have been studied, "extensive community-based immersion experiences, coupled with coursework [that helps prospective teachers interpret their experiences], seem to have the most promise" (2001, p. 102) for preparing white, middle-class prospective teachers for constructive engagement with student difference and diversity. But, she urges, we need research that examines what happens in practice during student-teaching and beyond. It is this challenge that *Diversity and the New Teacher* takes up. Welcome to a journey into largely uncharted territory.

PROLOGUE: A UNIVERSITY TEACHER CERTIFICATION PROGRAM

The prospective teachers we followed through their fall semester Field Experience and the first 8-week segment of their spring semester Student-Teaching at the same site were enrolled in a university teacher education program in a midsized metropolitan area in upstate New York. It is a postbaccalaureate certification program that is incorporated with a master's degree for prospective elementary teachers (2 years full-time) and can be combined with a master's degree for prospective secondary teachers (1 year full-time for certification only). Because of multiple sections of required courses and subject-area differences in secondary teacher education, there is, in effect, no single teacher education program at the university. Most prospective secondary teachers take educational psychology and social foundations courses, two literacy courses required by New York State, and subject-area methods-instructional strategies courses. Prospective elemen-tary teachers take methods courses in mathematics, science, and social studies as well as literacy (also known as reading and language arts). All prospective teachers complete a Field Experience course that involves at least 100 hours onsite at the assigned school, cohort meetings onsite with their university supervisor-mentor, and large-group meetings at the uni-versity, coordinated by the associate director. The following semester, pro-spective teachers complete two student-teaching placements and a Seminar in Teaching that involves both cohort and large-group meetings at the university.

According to their Web site, the certification program "is dedicated to preparing qualified, committed, and caring teachers who can work ef-fectively with students from various cultures with a wide variety of abili-ties and needs," and who can be "problem-solvers and critical thinkers who strive to self-reflect and improve their teaching" (retrieved August 24, 2007). The faculty and staff working with the program are described as "experienced educators with a commitment to excellence and lifelong learning." They include tenure track faculty, adjuncts, retired K–12 teachers and administrators, and doctoral students with teaching experience. At the time of this project, 2004–2006, approximately one-third of the staff was African American, Hispanic, or North African, and there was explicit attention to racial, ethnic, and cultural (including language and religion) diversity, social class, gender, and sexual orientation.

The program limited admissions and sought students with a GPA of at least 3.0 (out of 4.0), prior experience working with children or adolescents, good interpersonal and written communication, and openness to diversity. Key program themes included reflection and diversity, officially defined pretty much as I have done here. Prospective teachers completed a Reflective Inquiry Project, known as the RIP, involving both library and field research in their Field Experience school, about a question of interest to them. RIPs were to include a diversity dimension by including research literature from more than one racial/ethnic group, collecting data from diverse sources, and/or thoughtfully considering implications for diverse schools and groups of students. Diversity was part of most coursework in one way or another, treated differently by different instructors. New York requires that at least one student-teaching placement be in a "high-needs" district, defined in economic terms that frequently correlate with color.

In terms of the distinction Zeichner (1992) makes between teacher education programs that *infuse* multicultural or diversity concerns or *segregate* them in a separate course, this program represents moderate, uneven infusion. On his *fragmented* to *coherent* continuum, this program leans toward the fragmented with respect to diversity.

THE MAIN STAGES: TWO URBAN SCHOOLS

While I draw on the experiences of prospective and newer teachers across the United States and beyond, most of the cases and vignettes presented in subsequent chapters come from two schools in upstate New York: Royalton High School and Charter School. All proper names of schools, teachers and other school personnel, and prospective and newer teachers are pseudonyms. The prospective teachers at Royalton and Charter School selected their own pseudonyms; I have changed only a few to further protect anonymity.

School sites were selected from those in upstate New York where the university teacher education program described above places prospective teachers for Field Experience and Student-Teaching. Selection criteria were (1) urban sites with racially/ethnically diverse student bodies, where at least one "minority" group constituted at least 15% of the student population; (2) relatively "healthy" sites, i.e., those with a reputation for acting to minimize problems and respond constructively to those that do occur, better rather than worse intergroup relations, including teacher-student and teacher-administrator relations, and at least average academics for the school district; and (3) sites where both the school administration and university supervisor-mentor at the site were agreeable to participation in the project. I eliminated two urban high schools with academically selective admissions policies because experiences there could too easily be dismissed as atypical. That left one public high school with grades 9–12, Royalton, and one public charter school with grades K–5, Charter School.

Royalton has a proud history and strong traditions. Just a few years ago, it celebrated its 100th anniversary, and more than 1,000 alumni, spouses, faculty, and friends attended the celebratory dinner at a local convention center. The building itself is imposing and well maintained, though not at all modern. Set in a relatively quiet residential neighborhood with no adjacent sports fields, student parking lot, corner store, or strip mall, Royalton is surrounded by predominantly modest, generally well-kept, one- and two-family homes on small lots. Some have been divided into apartments, but there are no apartment buildings. A block or two in one direction is an area of larger, more expensive homes. Most students walk or take public transportation to and from the school.

At the beginning of the 2004–2005 school year, there were approximately 1,100 students at Royalton; by May 2005, there were approximately 900. Fifty-eight percent of the students were identified in school records as African American, 20% as Hispanic, 19% as white, and 3% as Native American. Among these students are a number of Middle Eastern and African Muslims and students for whom English is a second or third language. Data for the same school year show that 64% of the students qualified for free lunches and 8.5% qualified for reduced-price lunches. Most of the teachers and other school personnel are white; one assistant principal is African American.

A combination of changes within Royalton High School and its parent school district came together in the first year of our project, 2004–2005. Royalton, consequently, was a less healthy site than had been anticipated. I strongly doubt that more than a few school or university personnel realized the combined pressures on the school at that time. First, after a short period with an interim superintendent, the district had a new superintendent, one whose appointment was not uncontroversial. Second, the district's budget problems (closely tied to those of its city) had worsened, resulting in various cutbacks, including the closing of the Alternative High School for students with serious social-behavioral problems. Third, the school's female principal had retired, and a new principal, also female and with no prior experience as a principal, was appointed. Fourth, the district's school choice program was now fully in place, allowing students from all over the city to attend Royalton. Generally described as one of the better second-tier (i.e., nonselective) academic high schools in the city, Royalton now attracted students from varied neighborhoods, including one on the far side of the city whose high school was closed at the end of the previous year. As a result, the student population changed, and its various segments did not always get along well. So-called turf battles flared, as did adolescent tempers inflamed by gossip, particularly among female students. Although they involved a very small number of students, the violence was nasty at times, and media portrayals suggested and/or were interpreted as suggesting that Royalton was a dangerous place. Personally, I never felt threatened or fearful there. Royalton was far from chaotic like the urban high schools of film notoriety.

Within what seemed like days after the beginning of the 2004–2005 school year, the new superintendent and the longtime president of the teachers' union faced off in the first of what would be continuing confrontations, and some of the teachers were embroiled in controversy. The majority of both teachers and students, however, particularly the students, chose to stay out of the fray.

Most of the prospective teachers assigned to Royalton High School knew few of the specifics about Royalton or the district, beyond the presence of new leadership and continuing financial problems. They had little sense of the local context and history to frame and aid their interpretation of what they encountered directly or second-, third-, or fourth-hand in the teachers' workroom. Similarly, the prospective teachers assigned to Charter School knew few specifics about it other than its reputation for being well organized and "strict."

Charter School was in its fourth year of operation when our project began, located in an industrial corner of the city in an old building that has been extensively remodeled to provide light, airy classrooms and facilities. It also had about 1,000 students. In 2004–2005, 47% of the students were identified by the school as white, 40% as African American, 12% as Hispanic, and 2% as Native American. Data for the same school year show that 69% of the students were eligible for free (22%) or reduced-price (47%) lunches. Most of the faculty and other school personnel are white; the male principal is not.

Compared with Royalton, Charter School had more white students and fewer very poor students at the time of our project. The greater flexibility afforded charter schools did not affect engagement with student diversity in noticeable ways. I expect that school level (elementary) accounts for more of the differences between how prospective teachers at Charter School and Royalton High School responded to student diversity than does charter status, perhaps in large part because of the pressures to raise reading and math test scores in grades 3 through 8 associated with No Child Left Behind requirements. There are New York State Regents exams required for high school graduation, but the schools are not required to show "yearly progress" toward federal standards as are elementary schools.

THE NEW TEACHERS AND THE SUPPORTING CAST

We asked for volunteers among the prospective teachers (PTs) assigned to each school site to participate in our project by allowing us to sit in on their cohort meetings and their classes once they were teaching and agreeing to taped interviews (three, in most cases) about their experiences at the school during Field Experience and student-teaching. The first year, six PTs at Royalton and all four at Charter School agreed to participate. I returned to Royalton the following year, 2005–2006, to sit in and talk with a few PTs in order to test the representativeness of the first year's group of PTs. Although there did not appear to be a problem with representativeness, I found myself drawn in (I liked being at Royalton and was warmly welcomed back) and stayed on to include a second cohort of six more PTs at Royalton, for a total of 12 secondary and four elementary prospective teachers. The emphasis here is on Royalton and the new teachers there because they offer a greater range of experiences and responses to student difference and diversity.

The 12 Royalton PTs, five male and seven female, include one black male (Ethan); the others are white. They taught English, science, or social studies in grades 9, 10, 11, or 12. The four Charter School PTs, two male and two female, include one black female (Tammy); the others are white. They taught in grades K–1 to 5. Most of the 16 PTs attended public high schools in suburban or small-town districts. Malcolm and Rupert attended Catholic high schools; Malcolm described his as a Catholic military school. Tammy attended a city high school. Few had prior experience working with young people who are different from themselves in terms of race/ethnicity, socioeconomic status, or first language. Appendix B provides a listing of the PTs by school with their subject and/or grade levels.

A word about the supporting cast: Of the cooperating teachers (CTs), three at Royalton High School (all male, two social studies and one science) worked with PTs from our program both years; three of nine CTs are female;

one is an African American female. All four of the cooperating teachers at Charter School are female; one is Jamaican (she was not paired with the African American PT). They represent a mix of veteran and newer teachers. Both of the university supervisor-mentors are white retired teachers, one female who taught secondary foreign language, the other male who taught elementary grades and was an elementary school administrator for several years. Both thoroughly enjoy their work, earn their PTs' respect, and are still with the program. Although the elementary supervisor-mentor was relatively new to Charter School and has moved among elementary sites, the secondary supervisor-mentor has worked at Royalton for several years. She is widely known and well liked there.

OVERVIEW OF CHAPTERS 2–7

Chapter 2, "Getting Started at an Urban School," shows that prospective teachers, beginning as outsiders to the urban school sites at which they do their Field Experience and Student-Teaching, do not necessarily become insiders. Some remain uneasy guests. Others become interested visitors, while keeping their distance from both students and staff. A few learn enough about school and student cultures as well as individual students to get along and gain acceptance without giving up their goals for meaningful student learning and academic success.

Significantly, prospective teachers' "experience" or "knowledge" of the high school preceded their arrival insofar as they encountered the negative reputation of "city schools" from various sources once their urban placement was known. While some prospective teachers were more susceptible to the public's negative bias, all were at least a bit apprehensive about what they would encounter at Royalton High School. From illustrations of early experiences with the school and initial concerns that are highlighted here, one can begin to discern the various ways in which prospective teachers have approached or faced difference.

Chapter 3, "They Say, They Keep Telling Us," shows that the way in which prospective teachers engage (or avoid) student difference and diversity depends not only on their personal biographies or what they bring to the teaching situation, but also on influences at the school site, influences frequently referred to as "school culture" or "ethos." I use the language of "messages" to refer to the influences that prospective teachers encountered at Royalton High School, Charter School, and elsewhere. Messages to newcomers about "how we do things here" are not always received, and even if they are received, they are not always interpreted and acted upon as intended by the senders. By illustrating some of the "louder" or more widespread messages that prospective teachers reported and how they dealt with them, other new teachers can gain some ideas of what to expect in schools like these and begin to anticipate how they might deal with them.

Chapter 4, "Radical Individualism," is the first of three chapters that describes, illustrates, and analyzes various modes of engagement with student difference and diversity that emerged over time among prospective teachers at Royalton and Charter School and have been documented among new teachers elsewhere. "Radical Individualism," more evident among the prospective elementary teachers at Charter School, is a perspective that downplays, ignores, or avoids racial/ethnic/cultural, socioeconomic, and other group-linked differences because "everyone is different." Teaching should be individualized to a large extent, according to this view, because all students are unique.

"Radical Individualism" is a version of colorblindness that in practice tends to assume middle-class white norms and standards. Individual students may be given extra time and assistance (or enrichment activities), but the individualization remains relatively thin. Despite the rhetoric of individualization, priority is given to following school rules and meeting expectations for high(er) standards and standardized test scores. Whereas "Worlds Apart" (Chapter 5) suggests student pathology, "Radical Individualism" furthers conformity and basic skills much more than creativity, critical thinking, or cultural expression.

Chapter 5, "Worlds Apart," presents the perspective on engagement with difference and diversity that views Royalton High School and Royalton students as "not like us" or "not like me," where us/me refers to a white, middle-class, academically prepared, and cooperative if not well-motivated student standard. The student "others" at Royalton might be seen as interesting or "fun," but they require control, according to this view, before you can teach them anything. And then, it is best to use structured, teacher-dominated instructional methods not only to maintain control but also because of students' weak knowledge and skill base.

"Worlds Apart" illustrates an approach to difference and diversity that others have described as "illusory" schooling or teaching (Popkewitz, Tabachnick, & Wehlage, 1982), where teachers and students go through the motions but little is taught or learned, largely because students are not seen as ready or able to learn much or go very far in life. "Worlds Apart" reflects vestiges of deficit-remedial models and assumptions that were widespread from the 1960s to the 1980s. It is a way of surviving, of getting through the day, but not of succeeding in constructively engaging student difference and diversity to promote meaningful learning. In terms of broader social-political outcomes, "Worlds Apart" tends to maintain the status quo, including middle-class white privilege.

Chapter 6, "Bridging Different Worlds," also includes a variant that I call "Culture Shock and Accommodation." Both conscientiously attempt to communicate and connect with students different from oneself, "Bridging Different Worlds" with an academic emphasis and a bit more personal distance, and "Culture Shock and Accommodation" with a more personal or personalized emphasis. Most of the prospective teachers adopted a version of the bridging or accommodation perspective and strategy. This also is a relatively common strategy among newer teachers, as illustrated by Fred's experience at an urban middle school after teaching successfully at a selective high school in the city and a suburban Catholic school and then finding that his prior approaches and expectations just "didn't work" at Middle Academy.

"Bridging Different Worlds" is the most common and variable approach to engaging student difference and diversity among the prospective teachers we followed and among outstanding newer and experienced teachers studied by myself and others (e.g., Ladson-Billings, 1994). For prospective and newer teachers, this bridging doesn't just happen or happen as easily as may appear to be the case for experienced teachers. The cases presented here show teachers struggling to connect with their students, to find some common or neutral ground both personally and academically, and to communicate effectively. At least to some extent, that usually meant learning one another's language, even when that language is English. It means that the teachers move into previously unfamiliar territory, just as they are asking their students to do. They are not staying put, demanding that their students take all the risks and do all the work. The various forms of bridging and accommodation illustrated here offer hope for constructive engagement with student difference and diversity that brings meaningful student learning and teacher satisfaction. Whereas the shorter Chapters 4 and 5 can be seen as illustrating common pitfalls to be avoided, the longer Chapter 6 offers a range of more positive examples.

Chapter 7, "Where Do We Go from Here?", goes beyond summary to further consider the just-described patterns of engagement with difference and diversity. Their apparent assumptions and implications are considered in relation to the relevant literature, for example, that on culturally relevant or responsive teaching. Implications for teacher education and teaching are offered, for example, placing greater emphasis (and related resources) at the school sites where prospective teachers do their Field Experience and Student-Teaching in order to provide more guidance in making sense of and acting constructively within their situations. This is not simply a matter of college/university *or* school site emphasis and control, but of working together for the benefit of urban students and their teachers.

"Where Do We Go from Here?" offers implications for preservice and inservice teacher education policy and practice that run counter to, or cut across the grain of, several recent and ongoing movements in teacher education. Even with the best of intentions, loading more requirements on the "front end" of teacher education prior to initial teacher certification and teaching is not very helpful to constructively engaging difference and diversity. Hours, credits, and exams may appear to increase standards and rigor, but they miss the crucial criteria of practice on the ground, with students in schools. Instead of "more," there are clear implications in the cases and vignettes provided here for redirecting attention and the needed resources to the school sites where prospective teachers already are doing their Field Experiences and Student-Teaching in order to help them better engage student difference and diversity. How and how well are cooperating teachers and university supervisors working together in this regard? How many student-teacher evaluation forms include items regarding constructive engagement of student difference and diversity? How do teacher education programs select and prepare their cooperating teachers and student-teacher supervisors for helping prospective teachers constructively engage diversity? Questions such as these might well be considered when standards for teacher education policy and program accreditation are reviewed and revised.

The intended audience for this volume is *both* teacher educators and the prospective and newer teachers with whom they work. In some chapters (2 and 3, for example), I speak more directly to new teachers, while in other chapters (7, for example), my voice is directed more to teacher educators, administrators, and policymakers. My hope is that including more of us, in the colleges and the schools, in constructive dialogues about learning to teach the diverse groups of students in our schools will benefit all of us, especially our respective students.

2

Getting Started at an Urban School

Imagine yourself anticipating your field experience placement in a city school—sometimes called "urban" or "high needs" but always referring to a school with large numbers of students from lower socioeconomic status (SES) homes, many of whom are African American, Hispanic, or recent immigrants from various parts of the globe. You will be there for a semester and for your first student-teaching experience during second semester. How do you feel? What do you do by way of preparation? Perhaps you talk to friends or family, hoping for insider information from someone who has been there, even if it's second- or third-hand. Or maybe you get directions to the school and drive out to familiarize yourself with the area and where to park. Alternatively or in addition, you might try to keep an open mind as you wait until the morning when you are scheduled to meet the other members of your cohort and your university supervisor-mentor at the school for official introductions and the beginning of field experience.

Here, the focus is on the initial experiences of three cohorts of prospective teachers (PTs) with the urban schools where they were assigned for their Field Experience and first Student-Teaching placement. Other than personal accounts of one's teaching experience (e.g., Michie, 1999), the literature offers very little about getting started in an urban school, except perhaps for the cliché, "don't smile until Christmas," which is not very helpful and may be counterproductive. A notable exception is Weiner's (2006) account.

The Field Experience for these prospective teachers officially began about a month after the start of the university's fall semester in late August and a few weeks after the beginning of the public school year. The prospective teachers' "experience" or "knowledge" of the schools, especially the high school, preceded their arrival insofar as they encountered the negative reputation of most "city schools" from various sources especially after their assigned site was known. Most PTs were apprehensive beyond the usual concerns about doing well or simply surviving.

In contrast, there was much less anticipation of the elementary school site, one way or another, because it was relatively new, unfamiliar, and located on the edge of the city. It had not yet established a "reputation" beyond being highly structured. Consequently, the spotlight here is on the high school, Royalton, and the 12 English, science, and social studies prospective teachers we followed there during 2004–2005 and 2005–2006. Four PTs are highlighted in this chapter (Jaclyn, Ken, Lynn, and Mark): two male and two female, two who were among the more successful PTs by the end of their time at Royalton High School and two who were not. Their "stories," along with others, continue in the chapters that follow.

PRE-ENCOUNTER

I was a little nervous at first when I heard I was put in a, an urban school but, I mean, the kids there are a little more difficult than I expected at a suburban school, but it kinda adds a little more, um, excitement than kids sittin' around and listening, just, you know (Ken, science).

I had never heard good things about city schools (Lynn, science).

I really didn't know what to expect because I had never been in a, in a city school before. . . . So I just had to, like, see it for myself. I am one that doesn't try to make any kind of assumption whatsoever. I mean, you can read, you can read all different things, but you don't know what that one situation that you are placed in is going to be about (Mark, social studies).

I was scared. Well, it is a city school, and I hear all of these things about city schools, but I am not going to take them to heart (Mark).

I've definitely gained an experience I never thought I would have. Um, I never thought I would be, uh, in the position where I was going to an urban high school (Jaclyn, social studies).

I decided before I went there, I wasn't happy, but then, right before I got there, I just decided to just completely erase my mind of everything. Yes, I've heard negative things, but I've also heard positive things, and I really tried to grow within myself and find something that I could learn from. And if I hadn't done that, I probably wouldn't have been, wouldn't have learned anything, um, but I did. I went in with a blank mind, a clean slate, um, new students, new students, new teacher, and I really learned (Jaclyn).

> Pretty much everything I've heard outside of [Royalton High School], if I'm not talking to a teacher that's taught in a city school, it's negative (Jaclyn).

These excerpts from our conversations with the prospective teachers give some sense of their anticipation of a city or urban high school, even one with a proud history that we saw as having a diverse student body and healthy intergroup relations. It also was one where the university had regularly placed student-teachers for at least a half dozen years.

The interaction of individual and institution begins before the prospective teachers even arrive on-site for the first time. It is most evident when some PTs consider how they will deal with what has been portrayed as a difficult and/or dangerous situation. How nervous or scared they were initially turns out to be less important to constructively engaging diversity than what the PTs did about it. In this respect, Mark and Jaclyn were more proactive and positive than Ken and Lynn. Rather than just letting things happen, they reported trying not "to make any kind of assumption whatsoever" (Mark) and to go in "with a blank mind, a clean slate" (Jaclyn), despite their considerable apprehensions. Kaitlyn, an English PT, used similar language after saying that she was now "less scared than . . . the first day walking in." Asked what she had been scared about, she told me:

> Um, I don't know if scared is the correct term. Just all summer, well not all summer, since we found out that we were at [Royalton], I heard a lot of the various stereotypical, like, you know, "better watch out. It's a tough school." You know, "have your bullet proof vest." I never really heard anything positive from it, it was just everyone. [Royalton], downtown [city], you immediately get that reaction, so I didn't really know what to expect going into it, and I tried not to have any expectations. I didn't want to stereotype the school. I am, like, well obviously it can't be that bad. . . . I was just really unsure.

These comments came from family, people she worked with at the Red Cross, and friends.

In presenting prospective teachers' pre-encounter and encounter experiences and their accounts of their "greatest challenges," I purposefully minimize interpretive commentary, in part to "keep an open mind," as some of the PTs might say, and to avoid anticipating further information that has not yet been presented, but more importantly to encourage readers to note tentative parallels, patterns, connections with relevant literature, and "lessons" that might be learned. At the end of this chapter and throughout succeeding ones, my interpretive hand is more evident.

ENCOUNTER

The prospective teachers' initial experiences at Royalton High School appeared both to confirm some negative anticipations and allay others. "It's not so bad" pretty well summarizes their seemingly shared sense of relief. The teachers and staff were welcoming. Several PTs noted that their university mentor-supervisor knew a lot of people at the school and was welcomed back. Kaitlyn joked about her experience getting to Royalton the first time:

> I did not know how to get there. I have never been on the [interstate highway between the small city where she lives and Royalton]. I have never done any of that, so it was just really tense for me. I think I arrived an hour and 40 minutes early 'cus I didn't know how long it would take, and everyone's like "it will take you one and one-half hours from [her home]." Yeah, it takes you, like, 40 minutes if you get stuck in traffic. So, I left at about, like, 6 a.m., and I got there at 7. . . . I got a parking spot right up front too. I never had that space again. And I just got to walk around a little bit and, um, I talked to some of the students as they started to arrive to school. It was pretty nice.

Ken's comment about his expectations compared to his initial experiences was more direct than most. He told me:

> I guess I just had . . . a picture in my head of just troublesome kids that just cause problems all the time. I guess that's kind of a common stereotype of urban schools. And it, it does occur, but it's not as much as I pictured in my head.

During this early period, prospective teachers were getting to know the school and their likely cooperating teacher (CT), observing in several teachers' classes, and meeting regularly as a cohort with their supervisor-mentor, often in the school's library. Our field notes from these meetings indicate that a major message at the cohort meetings (and throughout the teacher education program, e.g., large-group Field Experience sessions) was about the importance of getting to know and understand your students so you can meet them where they are academically and speak their language. A teacher needs to connect with students, bringing subject matter into the students' world and terms, making it relevant so they will learn. Another continuing message was about diversity, beyond race or ethnicity, including culture (e.g., religion, language), ability, socioeconomic status, gender, and sexual orientation. Most PTs' initial awkwardness or discomfort in talking about difference, seemingly out of both ignorance and fear of offending someone (or appearing prejudiced or racist) seemed to fade over time as they got to know and become more comfortable with one another (and Royalton students) and their supervisor-mentor persisted in exploring aspects of difference and diversity with them through readings, activities, and discussion.

It was during this time that differences between the prospective teachers' high schools and Royalton High School seemed particularly salient. Reference to one's own high school experience is not surprising since most PTs had little or no other experience with secondary schools or students with which to compare or connect their Field Experience at Royalton. In our first conversations with the PTs, we asked specifically about how Royalton compared with their high schools. Three kinds of differences stood out: (1) student ancestry and socioeconomic status; (2) school resources; and (3) student knowledge, skills, and classroom behavior. The large majority of PTs were from middle- and upper-middle-class families and communities. Their high schools were predominantly or overwhelmingly white. Royalton, in contrast, was 15–20% white across the 2 years we were there, with 70% of the students reported as eligible for free or reduced-price lunches.

All 12 PTs acknowledged their minority status at Royalton, including Ethan, who did not like being seen and treated as African American. Ken told me that "almost the entire school is African American–Hispanic" whereas his suburban high school was "majorly white." Lynn described her school community as "pretty well-to-do" and also told me, "I have only on one other occasion have ever been put in with a group of people where I am one of the minority because only 19% of the school is white, so being on the other side, it's interesting." She did acknowledge that being a student-teacher and "hanging out" with your CT puts you in a position of authority that is different from being a minority student.

Mark described his suburban high school as "predominantly white" and Royalton as "predominantly African American." Jaclyn described her high school similarly and characterized Royalton as "not a very diverse school in terms of, you know, racial background." She continued, "It's, you know, the majority are African American students, um, there are some Asian students in the classes, there are some Indian students, um, and white students are minorities." Her racial minority status seemed to be a source of unease. The large majority of teachers at Royalton, however, were white, as Jaclyn recognized but did not seem to find reassuring. "I've never been in an urban city school where the majority of the kids are black and there are, like, two kids in the school that are white"—an obvious exaggeration in contrast to her earlier racial/ethnic breakdown of the student body.

Interestingly, she did not mention Hispanic students, predominantly Puerto Rican, who made up 23% of the student body in 2005–2006.

Along with racial and SES differences, prospective teachers noted differences in resources between their schools and Royalton, ranging from textbooks for students to paper for photocopying to extracurricular activities and sports facilities. Briefly, such resources were available in the PTs' schools and much less so at Royalton. A glaring example involves textbooks. English and social studies teachers at Royalton only had one class set of books for each course they teach (e.g., 9th-grade English, 11th-grade English). Regardless of what one might think of the quality of any or all textbooks, students are at a disadvantage when they cannot take a book home (or must see if one is available to use in study hall) to read or study for an exam. Amanda, a prospective English teacher, railed at the situation this way:

> [It] never would have been acceptable to me or to my parents if I was [a student] in a science lab that didn't have appropriate materials, um, or didn't have books to take home. Um, you know, the, the English classes, they don't have books. They, they read in class. The teacher hands out books at the beginning of the period and collects them back [at the end], and that never would have been acceptable in, in like, my school. That I couldn't have a textbook to take home or . . . appropriate science-type things because the resources just weren't there. That just never would have been an option.

She continued, describing the different ways that Royalton and her high school responded to the lack of materials.

> There was just always enough . . . but, if we'd been short on something either the school would've come up with the money for it or we would have some sort of a little fund-raiser and, and gotten it right away, but there's a lot of "making do" at [Royalton] with what they have, which is good and they, you know, teachers really do try hard and, but it's just a different mentality of, "Well, we just don't have it, and we're not going to get it." Um, you know, it's weird to think that I won't be able to assign homework, reading homework to my students . . . because they can't take the book home. . . . [W]hen I think about how much time I'm going to have to plan into lesson plans for just physically reading it . . . it lessens what you can do and how many activities you can do with students.

The disparities in resources between her affluent suburban high school and Royalton, the consequent differences in opportunity to teach and learn, and the "making do" attitude at Royalton were themes that Amanda returned to more than once.

Ken, a prospective biology teacher, seemed more resigned to the lack of resources. "Unfortunately," he told me, "the classroom that I worked in didn't even have a working sink or anything else. So, it's just, you, it takes such an effort to do any kind of experiment in front of the class because you just have nothing to work with." When I asked Ken, "How are you at scrounging?," he responded, "Well, I mean, you can get water, you just gotta go out of your way [halfway down the hall, he said later], fill up a bucket of water in another room and bring it in and just kinda, just takes a little more time and effort. You just gotta figure out how to bring the materials in." Ken seemed to have mixed feelings about whether he should invest that time and effort.

Whereas Amanda was angry and seemed to be trying to work around the lack of books for students to read and study from outside of class, Ken seemed to be giving in with little resistance. By our second conversation, Ken had found that the school had two video projectors and used one with his CT's laptop to show short clips from the Internet. Still, Ken lamented "but besides that, it's still basically just using the white board during class . . . and then I put up the notes afterwards on the overhead projector." He said that he'd only done one experiment over the 8 weeks, so he didn't have "to deal with running back and forth to get water so much, but, I mean, it still takes away from things you could do" to foster student interest and understanding. "I don't teach lab," he said. "I'm not really supposed to do experiments, but it helps to teach if you use, kind of, examples." A few minutes later, he recalled another experiment requiring water that he had done with three of his classes (the others were too unruly, he said) to increase the relevance of their study of respiration:

> for respiration, since it has to do with, like, converting oxygen to carbon dioxide and stuff, I actually had them running around the school and, and breathing into stuff that shows the increase in carbon dioxide [a blue solution that turns green and then yellow with carbon dioxide, and changes color faster with more carbon dioxide]. So I had them kinda do exercise so they realize how that works. . . . [T]hey liked it.

However, Ken said, "I had to use that water again. . . . I filled up a huge pitcher of the stuff, though, so I didn't have to go back for it."

PTs emphasized differences between their own high school classmates' and Royalton students' knowledge, skills, and behavior. Several acknowledged that they were in honors and AP (Advanced Placement) classes and did not mix much with students in regular classes. Now that Kaitlyn has done some substitute teaching at the high school she attended, she said, "it was all there, the culture difference, the diversity, it was all in the school, but I just didn't see it." She continued:

> So, it really seems like a completely different school to me, um, looking in the hallways, and I tried to convince myself, "oh well, it must not have been like this when I was there" [4 years ago] but that's not true at all. Learning about, just about the drugs in the school. I was so naïve to that going through high school, I had no idea. And you can get it from people's lockers and down the street after school. I have been hearing all this conversation between students in the classroom, and it just floors me 'cus . . . we didn't have those conversations. So, they just talk about, um, you know, who's pregnant, who's in court, who got arrested, what fight happened, and that's similar to [Royalton] conversations in the hallways, their social lives.

Not surprisingly, PTs were unfamiliar, and probably uncomfortable, at least initially, with students whose prior knowledge and reading-writing-math skills were weak. Having been "good" students, they also were challenged by students who were disruptive or simply didn't seem to care about schoolwork. While Lynn listed substantial differences between Royalton and her affluent suburban high school with "a lot of academically minded people," including herself, she recognized that "I cannot expect them to be like me or what I have known or experienced in the past, so it is kind of wakening that up." From his observations of classes and students at Royalton, Ken said "I noticed a lot of students don't care very much. . . . [A] lot of students just sat there and didn't copy notes, put their heads down, and just didn't really put any effort into doing anything."

That some prospective teachers might have been misinterpreting some of their students' "not caring" behavior is suggested by Amanda's concern with "students who believe they just can't do it," that "I'm not smart enough," or "it doesn't matter." She told me, "so I think making it [English] matter to them is probably, like, the first goal." When students just sit there, don't copy notes, put their heads down, and don't "really put any effort into doing anything," are they showing that they "don't care very much" (Ken) or "believe they just can't do it," that "I'm not smart enough," or "it doesn't matter" (Amanda), or some combination or something else? More successful PTs tended to test their assumptions about students and tried to keep an "open mind."

EMERGING CONCERNS, CHALLENGES

In our first conversations with prospective teachers, we asked what they saw as their greatest challenges at Royalton High School and the elementary Charter School. We also prompted PTs to say more about each challenge they mentioned and how they might deal with it. Their most frequently voiced concerns involved relationships with students: connecting with students, personal emphasis (eight PTs); connecting with students, academic emphasis (five); classroom management or control, apart from personal or academic relationships (six). Other concerns or challenges mentioned by at least four PTs were student engagement, teaching differently from one's CT, teaching well, and daily planning. These concerns are similar to those voiced by prospective teachers in other times and places.

The prospective teachers at Royalton (11 of 12) were particularly concerned about establishing and maintaining positive relationships with students different from themselves as a means of enhancing classroom management, student learning, and their own sense of accomplishment or satisfaction. In contrast, the PTs at the Charter School voiced more substantive curriculum concerns related to what they perceived as the school program's structure and intensity. Twelve of the 16 PTs mentioned communicating or connecting with students as one of their greatest challenges, 11 of the 12 PTs at Royalton and one at the Charter School.

At or near the end of the student-teaching placement at Royalton and the Charter School, we asked prospective teachers about the challenges they had mentioned earlier. In this section, I draw on their comments to describe and illustrate the challenges most clearly relevant to *Diversity and the New Teacher* and then begin to show different trajectories in PTs' responses. These different trajectories then become the focus of later chapters. Most clearly relevant to *Diversity and the New Teacher* are the challenges involving relationships with students, student engagement, and classroom management. Although each category has a different emphasis, the categories are not mutually exclusive. The prospective teachers who mentioned each are indicated in Table 2.1.

Three of the four prospective teachers who mentioned student engagement as a challenge also mentioned either personal or academic connections with students, but none mentioned classroom management as a separate concern. All five Royalton PTs who mentioned classroom management as a challenge also mentioned personal or academic connections with students (three each, with Cora mentioning both). Dante's concern with classroom management at the Charter School was specifically about how to control or discipline without being intimidating. His overriding

Table 2.1. Greatest Challenges

	Personal Connection	Academic Connection	Student Engagement	Classroom Management
Amanda		X	X	
Cora	X	X		X
Dante				X
Ethan	X			
Jaclyn	X			
Kaitlyn	X		X	
Kate		X		X
Ken		X		X
Kirk	X			
Lynn	X			X
Malcolm			X	
Mark	X			X
Renee	X		X	
Rupert		X		

concern was with being a male elementary teacher of college football player size and proportions.

Connecting with Students—Personal

Communicating and connecting with students (personal emphasis) was described by prospective teachers in terms of getting to know the students, establishing positive teacher-student relationships, and sparking students' interest in learning. Jaclyn, for example, talked about the importance of "understanding the students and letting them into . . . my life" because students "need to, like, feel a connection with someone, and I've understood that now. It's just a concern of mine that they won't, almost that they won't let me into their world and their lives." She also seemed concerned about how much to tell them about herself. Her goal, she said, was that "we can kind of create more of a community" within their classroom. She told me:

> It's definitely going to be hard. I realize that, but I feel like—the only way that they'll learn and the only way that they will be interested in walking into my classroom in the day is if they feel like they can be open and, you know, share things and ask questions and feel like I am not going to put them down or make them feel, you know, stupid or dumb for asking these questions.

Later, she recalled that:

> in the beginning, just learning their names, just knowing their names is huge, because they don't think you know their name. . . . They would be, like, "Ah! How do you know my name? . . . like, I can't believe you know my name, how does she know my name?" And it was just like, "now, I'm holding you accountable."

Another example involved "the thing where you stand in the hallway in between classes, you stand at the door at the end of class, the beginning of class, welcoming students, saying goodbye." Jaclyn related that

> I think it made a huge difference. . . . If I had been speaking with them, prior to class starting or in the hallway, and I got to know them better, I think in class they respected me more. I could also pull things out of my hat that I had just been talking to them about in the hall . . . to get their attention back in the classroom. I would say something that I knew would catch their attention so, um, we could focus more on what I wanted to do.

Pulling "things out of my hat" also showed that Jaclyn was listening to and remembering what her students were saying, which probably made a positive impression on them (akin to her learning their names). I was struck by how far Jaclyn had moved beyond her initial apprehension about being placed in a majority African American school where whites like herself were in the minority.

While recognizing the importance of positive relationships with students, Lynn seemed hesitant about taking initiatives like those Jaclyn reported. She described herself as "not a great first impression kind of person. . . . [Y]ou got to get to know me a little bit because I am on the quiet side." Lynn didn't return directly to the challenge of communicating and connecting with students in later conversations. Her focus narrowed to classroom management and planning for teaching. Although she may have heard the same messages as Jaclyn about the importance of connecting with students, Lynn responded differently.

Mark provides a third case of how PTs deal with the challenge of communicating and connecting personally with students different from themselves. His examples span personal and academic emphases. Mark expressed concern about relating to students because their backgrounds differed from his. He talked about learning from his students, showing that he cared about them, and trying to make his social studies classes relevant so they wouldn't be boring. Getting students involved and interested in his classes, he said, "kinda relates to, um, relating to them and making things relevant to them in order for them to become interested in it." Among the ways Mark identified for learning more about his students and relating to them were getting to know his students individually, connecting current and past events, and being responsive to student questions. He concluded, "if you take that extra step [to learn about and from your students], I think that the, the students will realize that you actually are, you know, showing that you do care."

Mark also talked about having higher expectations for students and prompting them to think critically. "I think that, um, you know, sometimes you need to push the students, to challenge them a little bit and that makes them more interested and, you know, hopefully makes them wanna try and do better." While Mark's beliefs and experience might not be endorsed by most social studies teachers, they are consistent with research about challenging social studies classes (e.g., Stevenson, 1990).

In contrast to Lynn, whose concerns about relating to students personally shifted to an emphasis on classroom management, Mark no longer seemed concerned about classroom management. By the second semester, Mark's focus on relating to students and making the subject matter relevant was even stronger. If you do that, discipline follows, he told me. He recalled being worried about relating to students at Royalton because their backgrounds were so different. Initially, he said:

> I was just like, "OK, hopefully I'm decent enough where I can keep their attention." Um, and that the relationships will come along, like, 'cus the whole thing kind of, I don't know, kinda links into classroom

management. The whole thing, like our teachers told us, "Just, just teach, you know. . . . [I]f you worry too much about disciplining, you're going to lose sight of what you are really there to do. You're not a babysitter, you are there to teach them things." I tried to go on that concept too. And so, um, that worked out well.

Connecting with Students—Academic

Communicating and connecting with students (academic emphasis) was described by PTs in terms of getting students settled down and keeping them on task, getting students to (want to) come to class, and relating classwork to student interests. Getting to know one's students and establishing positive teacher-student relationships (personal emphasis) were lower priorities or means to an end. Ken, Kate, and Cora provide an illustration of this "challenge" and possible responses.

Initially, Ken sounded like Mark at a lower key or energy level. Because the students and the school differed from Ken's more affluent, predominantly white, suburban high school and his experience in advanced classes, he told me "you just need to put in an effort to connect with the students and get to know them," more so than in more familiar settings. He said that "trying to get the students engaged in the lesson" was one of his greatest challenges, after "controlling the students." He said, "So, I think you need to, kinda, connect with them, and that also helps to get them interested in a lesson, if you can get the lesson to connect with some kind of stuff that they're interested in, then they'll be interested in what you're teaching." You also should be friendly and show interest in the students. Otherwise, Ken said, students are "not gonna pay attention, they're not gonna care that much." An example Ken offered was the questionnaire that he asked students to complete about their interests. He was surprised that "a lot of them have the kind of interests that I had, very similar. . . . [T]hey like talking on the phone and watching movies and playing sports, so it's still your typical high school students." This seeming turnaround in Ken's thinking was temporary, in part perhaps because it was based on "interests" more than personal or life experiences.

Since he was teaching biology, Ken also considered doing some experiments "that'll, like, fascinate them, that'll make them more interested in learning about it." But, he said, "it takes such an effort to do any kind of experiment in front of the class because you just have nothing to work with." Recall Ken's frustration with the nonworking sink in his classroom and having to carry in water.

Later, Ken, like Lynn, had come to focus on classroom management. Making the content relevant to students has "just been real hard," he said.

The respiration experiment that Ken described to us was well received by students, but he had to go "halfway down the hall" to get the needed water. Getting the students' respect, however, wasn't a problem. Age was not the issue he thought it might be. As an example, he said, "well, they curse a lot, but when I do tell them not to, they apologize. . . . [T]hey don't even realize they do it, it's kind of part of their regular language." Teaching the class as a whole, however, was difficult for Ken, and he seemed to have redefined the problem or challenge from connecting with students to controlling them.

For Kate, a prospective science teacher in the classroom next to Ken, connecting with students primarily for academic purposes was linked to her desire to involve them in more thought-provoking activities than her CT employed. She hoped that her students would respond well to the new things she wanted to try. Looking toward student-teaching, she said, "I'm scared but, like, I'm really excited." Getting to know and getting along with Royalton students was less a concern for Kate than using that relationship for meaningful academic learning. Like Malcolm (the only Royalton PT who did not cite connecting with students as a challenge), Kate seemed at ease at Royalton. She told me:

> I like the kids that I'm working with a lot. I've gotten to know some of them, just, you know, working in the class, I've helped 'em out with labs or assignments or things like that. . . . [T]hey just all have pretty cool personalities and I just, I'm excited to get to know them and to finally be up there and doing it instead of just watching it be done.

Later, when I asked what she was looking forward to most, Kate paused and then said something similar:

> I think just forming a relationship with the students because now that I've gotten to talk to some of them, just like a few words here and there, you know, . . . I think the kids are really cool, and they just have very unique personalities, and . . . I just wanna, like, get in there and see how they respond to me. That's what I'm excited about.

As an example, Kate described a male student who is "very animated during class," is "really entertaining," asks and responds to questions, is "usually paying attention and doing what he's supposed to do and still having fun," and "does really well."

Kate told me that she saw her greatest challenge at Royalton as "finding a way to get the kids motivated . . . wanting to do, do work, wanting to learn, getting excited, getting them to participate." Instead of her CT's lecturing, notes, and worksheets, Kate talked about "trying to get them to respond, trying to get them to start thinking and answering more complicated questions . . . bring in more activities for them to do and just get them more engaged, get them more actively involved" and figuring things out for themselves.

By second semester, Kate had had opportunities to try out various activities—with mixed results. She said, "So, I definitely feel like I was very successful . . . at times and, of course, sometimes it just, like, blew out the window." "At first," she said, "it was the challenge of just getting them to do it, because obviously they haven't been used to it, and all they would do is take notes and do handouts. . . . I just had to, like, get on them every single second and be, like, 'do this, do this, do this,' and maybe eventually they'll do it." Picture a young woman, slim and of medium height, quietly attractive with a soft voice, simply persisting and not giving up on her students.

When I asked, "What did you do? Literally badger and hound them?" Kate responded, "yeah, pretty much . . . go around to every kid and every group and be, like, 'do this, get this done.' And, you know, I didn't yell and . . . mostly I'd just kind of, would talk to them . . . just constantly, would not get out of their face until they did it." Once the students became accustomed to Kate and the more demanding activities, "for the most part, again once you got them going, they would accomplish it" and do well. If Kate had not established good relationships with her students, it is unlikely that she would have been able to get them to do more than the rote work her CT emphasized. In some ways, classroom management was more challenging than in a traditional classroom, as Kate's CT had warned, while in others it was less so because students were more engaged, even if somewhat noisily at times. It was clear from Kate's account that her CT discouraged the kinds of activities she used and advised her just to tell the students what they needed to know for the state exam.

A third example of connecting with students primarily for academic purposes is provided by Cora, like Ken and Kate, a prospective science teacher. She also saw connecting with students with a more personal emphasis as a challenge and, like Kate, wanted to teach differently than her CT in what she called a "more student-centered" way. The academic challenge was to "spark their interests . . . getting them to want to pay attention and do their work and come to class. . . . I wanna try to find some sort of way to get them excited for at least 42 minutes a day. That's all I want." "You can see all of the potential just by watching them" she told me, but attendance is a major problem. Several PTs echoed the attendance-absentee problem at Royalton. (When I was out at the school one Thursday in late April 2006, I noticed an absentee list on the office counter and saw that more than one-third of the students were absent.)

For Cora, who attended high school in a small town in western New York after living in rural areas in South Carolina and Virginia, Royalton was a major change. After "just seeing the students and interacting with them," she found that "they're just high school kids, just trying to get through high school and get on with their lives. . . . [T]hey are just people, so I didn't think I had anything to be afraid of really." "Getting to know the kids" was one of the things she was looking forward to most. She told me, "there are kids in there that I am, like, 'wow, that kid is really smart!' . . . of course you got the kids who fall asleep and things like that. . . . [I]n general, I am really impressed by the students . . . they are all unique, like, they can all teach me something, and hopefully I can teach them something."

Student Engagement

Apart from connecting with students, the challenge of engaging students in school learning, making it matter to them, and believing they could do it despite, in some cases, a weak knowledge or skill base, was cited by four PTs, two English (Amanda, Kaitlyn) and two social studies (Renee, Malcolm). Amanda, for example, told me:

> I really think the biggest challenge is the students who believe they just can't do it. . . . [A] lot of the students there [at Royalton, compared to her high school] sometimes feel, "I just can't do it, I'm not smart enough," or "it doesn't matter." . . . [F]or some students, they're like, "I don't care, it doesn't matter, it doesn't matter what grade I get," you know, "I just need to get by." So I think making it matter to them is probably, like, the first goal.

Amanda cited a student in one of her 11th-grade English classes who is pregnant with twins, saying:

> [I]t's hard to tell a pregnant 16-year-old that reading a poem by Walt Whitman's gonna matter in her life. . . . [T]he two things I really try to focus on are how important in life being able to communicate is, that it's such an important part of every single aspect from getting a job to, to figuring out how to read the back of the [infant] formula can. . . . [N]o matter what their interests are, in some way they're gonna need to communicate [verbally and in writing].

Amanda described the second thing she tries to focus on as showing students how "even the oldest literature, plays and poems, connect to, to things that are current and, and to things that are going on in their life." As an example, she said, "we're gonna kinda stem off Thoreau's writings in civil disobedience and try to relate it to, like, Martin Luther King and Malcolm X and . . . then tie it into some current things." "I'm hoping to kind of teach them that, you know, that they can do it, they can stand up and make that difference."

Later in the school year, Amanda was still concerned about "the apathy of the kids who just didn't care," which she described as "the most difficult part, at least for me as a teacher." She had not been as successful as she'd hoped:

> The one thing, like, I just never did figure out how to get around . . . just trying to find individual students' motivation. It was really hard to find universal things. But, you know, to find some reason for that particular student, why they needed English. . . . I tried to find things that would interest them, 'cus if you can suck them in for a couple days . . . you can get them in the pattern, um, but a lot of times, you know, what would happen is, you have somebody who, like, for a week or something would really care, but something else would happen. Whether it be at home or a fight or, you know, something, and they would be discouraged, and it would just carry over into all of their classes. So, I kinda tried to keep reminding [them] why it was important in the bigger picture.

Despite an encouraging CT and some notable successes (e.g., with her 9th graders and *Romeo and Juliet*), Amanda concluded that:

> the overall, like, general sense of apathy was just, like, so pervasive, I never did find a way, and partially 'cus it is pervasive through the faculty and staff and the administration, and it was just so completely, it was throughout, the whole school was just surrounded by, it was really hard to get around it.

Amanda's CT seemed to play a key role in her not giving up. Her CT had high expectations for the students, Amanda said, "and expected them to understand things, and she really tried to expose them to a lot of things. . . . [S]he didn't really give up, where I saw other teachers, like, give up. She really stuck with what she wanted to teach and . . . you saw students, like, that it reached." (For the record, the student pregnant with twins is, I learned later, Polish, and Amanda's cooperating teacher is African American.)

A second case is provided by Malcolm, who said that his biggest challenge is "getting the students to want to learn, getting them to want knowledge, to crave knowledge and to just want to make it their own." In response to my question about his ideas for doing that, Malcolm talked about being patient, taking things slowly, putting the subject matter in their terms and individualizing so that students are "getting it" and "explaining it," and putting some pressure on the students so that they work things out (e.g., alliances in World War I). He gave an example from his 10th-grade global history class involving map-reading and learning how to use a "key" or "legend."

> So, just by looking at a map they can learn something. "Yeah, we learned this," and they could explain it to me. Um, and repeat it back, and I really didn't give them the answer, but they had to kinda come up with it themselves. I think that that's the first step 'cause I saw a little sparkle in their eye, little, little glint, um, specifically the one girl who kept on saying, "Mister, Mister . . . um, I'm stupid, dumb, why do you keep on asking this? No, I don't know. Ask her [refering to another student]." And I was working with three girls. I said, "No, I'm just gonna keep on, I'm gonna stay right with you until you get this." And by the end she said all that back to me, and she just kinda smiled, and it was positive.

Small steps and successes like this encouraged Malcolm to continue to help his students build their knowledge and skills as a basis for further learning. He told me, "some of the feedback I got from students definitely showed me that they were valuing that experience, and I hope that's what happens everyday. It's not, but . . . I think we can do some really interesting things, and I think they can grasp a lot . . . starting with the little steps." Although Malcolm might be seen as going "back to basics," he had no intention that he or his students would remain there.

Classroom Management

"Classroom management" is my preferred language, shared by a few prospective teachers, whereas others spoke of discipline or "control," as in controlling the students or their classroom. Included here are the six PTs whose initial concerns about classroom management were mentioned apart from connecting with or engaging students. Four of the six were science PTs. Social studies PT Mark concluded that discipline follows from relating to students and making the subject matter relevant, and earth science PT Kate continued to find classroom management challenging but maintained her focus on active student learning. Lynn and Ken, on the other hand, seemed to subordinate connecting with students to management-control. Cora's management concerns lessened as she got to know her students and gained experience and confidence.

Prospective and student-teachers have long been concerned about management-control-discipline. Initial management concerns for Royalton High School PTs were likely exacerbated by unfamiliarity with diversity and students different from themselves and fear stemming from ignorance and/or prejudice. Connecting with students with a personal emphasis (the challenge most often cited by PTs) can be seen as a way of heading off or alleviating management problems. The importance of relating to or connecting with students was a regular and perhaps frequent message both in university teacher education coursework and at Royalton High School. Less frequent and largely from university coursework was the message that Mark echoed about discipline following from relevant planning and instruction. There were, of course, countermessages equivalent to "lay down the law from day one and enforce it," largely from some Royalton teachers.

As indicated earlier, Ken's initial concern about connecting with students for academic reasons gave way to a preoccupation with control. He said that controlling the students was "still a challenge . . . if not even more than it was before." Even though he had gotten to know the students, and they him, Ken said:

> It's still hard to control certain students. . . . [I]t's people talking during class, people not paying attention. . . . [A] lot of the kids just don't care, so they won't take notes, they won't even take their tests, they just hand in their tests blank. Just, mostly just interrupting the class and talking to each other. . . . [T]he main thing is, just the talking more than anything.

In addition to the ideas for connecting with students that Ken mentioned earlier, he also told me:

> I think . . . you just need to . . . show that you're the boss in the class when you first get up there. . . . [I]f I get up there, and they're not showing respect, I need to prove to them that I'm gonna do something about it. . . . [M]y teacher [CT] recommended, he's like, "If you need to, you warn them about something, and if they don't listen, you make an example of one person, toss 'em out of class, do whatever you have to do. Just show them that you're willing, that you're able to do what you want, and you will act on it. You're not just up there to teach and have no authority."

Noteworthy here are assumptions about the desirability of a didactic (e.g., "get up there," "taking notes") and largely authoritarian (e.g., "the boss," "toss 'em out") mode of teaching that is at odds with "connecting with students."

By his second semester at Royalton, Ken seems to have adopted his CT's recommendations. He told us that control came from:

> Just threatening to throw 'em out and write them up is basically, that works. Threatening to keep them after school works. . . . As soon as you tell 'em that you're gonna write them up, they don't necessarily listen, but as soon as you pull out that slip that you're gonna fill out, then they listen right away. . . . And if you write up one person . . . or kick 'em out or something, it seems, it kinda quiets down the rest of the class too.

And bellwork [a short assignment right at the beginning of class] had become a daily quiz based on the previous day's class because, Ken said, "it's hard to get their attention." If students paid attention, the quiz should be easy, he told us, but "unfortunately, it's pretty hard for most of them since half of them don't pick up what I teach them. They don't pay attention." These quizzes may be the tests that Ken said some students were turning in blank. It is unclear from his account whether the quizzes helped to resolve the "attention" problem, generated resentment that increased the "not caring" problem, or something else.

"I kinda go with just the rules of the cooperating teacher" Ken told us, but "students don't seem to understand what the rules are, though . . . and I'm like, '[S]orry. That's the rules. I can't do anything about it. I don't make the rules up.'" By "don't seem to understand," Ken is saying that students "don't follow" the rules, since, if they understood the rules, he assumes that they would follow them, as he presumably did when he was in high school. Further, Ken is telling students that he is not responsible for making the rules, just enforcing them.

Ken saw his CT as "one of the stricter teachers," and appreciated his CT's assistance with discipline, saying, "I've gotten a lot from my cooperating teacher. He's helped me a lot with that." Ken also agreed with his CT's complaints about school discipline policies and the assistant principal's discretion in handling students who have been "written up" and sent to "the office." He told us, "I don't really like the way they run things with the principals and all that."

Ken concluded that:

> discipline problems just keep me from teaching. I feel like when I'm in front of the class I'm spending more time tryin' to get kids to be quiet

and kids to do stuff than I am actually teaching. Like every time I start teaching, I have to deal with some other student talking, that I have to turn around and tell him to be quiet and all that kind of stuff.

In the class I observed Ken teaching, he was literally in front of the class, with the black science lab table separating him from his students. There were students talking and looking at school yearbooks as well as responding to and asking questions.

Interestingly, by the end of his student-teaching at Royalton, Ken said that control became less of a problem as he got to know his students. With seeming surprise he added, "Um, I guess they, they did like doing activities more than sitting there and taking notes and stuff, and working in groups usually kind of helped with them. They paid attention more, but they were still a little more talkative and everything." "But," he continued, "I think also you just needed to be strict with them, and they need to know that if they're going to do something wrong, they're going to get kicked out of class, or, you're gonna call their parents or something."

Ken's apparent conflict between student engagement and control is evident. His CT did not advise him in advance about how to teach, he said, just what to cover, and then provided feedback afterward, with an emphasis on classroom management. "His feedback was really good," Ken said, "that was, like, the best part about him. Plus he was very honest and everything . . . it was helpful. He told me, like, what I could do to change things and stuff like that." Ken mentioned that instructors in the teacher education program at the university advocated using different methods, but "it's just kinda hard to do all that . . . especially with the students that I had, it was hard to really use too many different kinds of methods." At the same time, he recognized that the students "did like doing activities." He said, "I guess I always felt like I wanted students to, uh, like, enjoy the teaching and everything, but at the same time, like, learn stuff, and I think that was also something that was kinda difficult to get."

Classroom management was at the top of Lynn's list of challenges, as it was for Ken. "I don't have a big, bellowing voice, not yet anyway," she told me. "I am not sure yet how I am going to say, 'OK, we gotta get working now,' and just keeping people on track and that sort of thing." Lynn mentioned the bellowing or "bellowy" voice several times, apparently referring to her CT, who could and did bellow. She recognized management alternatives, but expressed concern that they might not work, and said, "I kind of want to be consistent."

By our second conversation, Lynn was emphasizing consistency and seemed to echo her CT's concerns about inconsistent rule enforcement at the school level, which she referred to as "chaos and craziness," meaning not orderly.

> I keep hearing, you know, there is no penalty for having a cell phone, for having a hoodie, for having all these things that they aren't supposed to do, and even if you get detention and you don't show up, it doesn't matter, nothing happens to you. You know, just kind of results in chaos, and there are so many teachers that let this slide that, um, things keep happening.

And, she said, this inconsistency and lack of consequences makes it more difficult for teachers who do (try to) enforce the rules.

Meanwhile, Lynn seemed relieved that her CT indicated that it wasn't necessary for her to bellow: "It was just nice because he said that, you know, 'use something other than bellowing,' because I can't bellow like he can. So, the fact that he, like, directly said, you know, 'do some of this, try this or that.' . . . So, I was very happy about that." She continued, "I am feeling like I am going to have to come up with a plan, explain the plan, and make sure everybody knows about it, and then enforce it, but if I do it's not terrifying." Being scared, Lynn told us, was not about Royalton, "but just with teaching in general" and all the planning and preparation required. Compared to Ken, Lynn seemed surprised more than put off by the amount of hard work that teaching requires.

Things got better with respect to classroom management, Lynn told us during our third conversation, but she should have been firmer sooner. Continuing her tendency toward dramatic language, Lynn said, "I got trotted over many, many times. It's like they put on cleats and just ran over my body that had fallen over because I didn't have enough discipline in there and management. So you need discipline to survive." She noted that "the kids that I had problems with gave problems to my [cooperating] teacher too, so definitely by throwing people out more at the beginning, I think it would have been better. . . . [I]t was the same kids over and over." Her account prompts me to wonder about the efficacy of "throwing people out" if "it was the same kids over and over" who were disruptive in class.

Lynn then returned to the "kind of person" she is. "I am not a tough person so actually to do it [be tough regarding discipline] was hard." Rather than yelling and threatening, Lynn said:

> I am more, like, "let's compromise and deal with it" instead of, you know, "you're a pain, and you have to sit down now or you gotta go," and maybe start by asking them "will you please sit down" . . . but it

was just like, if you don't sit down the first five times, I don't have any other option but to kick you out or tell you to sit down in less than a nice way. I am not always going to say "please" if you're not responding.

Lynn's ambivalence also was evident in her looking back and saying that "I would have kicked some people out very early on, just to say, 'hey, you're bothering me, you have to get out of here.' I am not sure if I could have done that very early on. I probably could not have. I am not even sure I could really do it now to be honest."

She said that she was still working on "lay[ing] down the law": "I am just used to dealing with a little bit of noise level because they are never all going to be quiet at [Royalton]. Well, they were occasionally, but I got to work on stomping my foot down there too." Recall Lynn's statement about where she comes from, hard work, and responsibility. Earlier, she was working hard as a student and taking responsibility for learning. Now she is expected to make the transition to the teacher's role, working hard at both classroom discipline and lesson planning.

CONCLUSIONS

From pre-encounter to encounter experiences at Royalton High School, to prospective teachers' emerging concerns, one can begin to see at least sketchy outlines of how these PTs faced difference and engaged student diversity as well as the more general challenges of teaching. All four PTs whose experiences I have highlighted in this chapter (Jaclyn, Ken, Lynn, and Mark) had very little direct or personal contact with people different from themselves or high schools different from their own before walking through the doors of Royalton. The paths they followed or cleared, however, differed in important ways.

Some tentative interpretations seem warranted at this point. First, pre-encounter and early encounter experiences and feelings are not necessarily a reliable indicator of where PTs are heading. For example, Jaclyn's initial unfamiliarity and fears about urban schools and students were substantial, especially being one of the white minority at Royalton. Yet she moved toward very constructive and satisfying engagement with difference and diversity, as did Mark, a trajectory I call "Bridging Different Worlds." How she and other PTs accomplished this transition or metamorphosis is examined in Chapter 6.

Second, the interaction of individual and institutional influences regarding engagement with difference and diversity is becoming apparent. Ken and Lynn, for example, had the same CT (in different years), and both were swayed by his disciplinary beliefs and practices. Yet Ken appeared to endorse and conform more than Lynn. A different mix of individual and institutional influences is evidence in Kate's persistence in actively involving her students despite her CT's repeated discouragement.

Finally, at least three strategies employed by PTs to deal with difference and diversity can be distinguished. "Radical Individualism," more evident among Charter School PTs, tends to downplay or ignore racial/ethnic/cultural, socioeconomic, and other differences among groups of students because everyone is different, all individuals are unique (Chapter 4). "Worlds Apart" sees Royalton High School and Royalton students as "not like us" or "not like me," where us/me refers to a white, middle-class, cooperative student standard (Chapter 5). "Bridging Different Worlds," including a variant I call "Culture Shock and Accommodation" (Chapter 6), conscientiously attempts to communicate and connect with students different from oneself, either with an academic emphasis and a bit of distance or with a more personal emphasis. Most of the PTs adopted a version of the bridging or accommodation strategy (e.g., Mark, Jaclyn). "Worlds Apart" was a less common, and less successful, strategy (e.g., Ken, Lynn).

Importantly, across strategies employed for dealing with difference and diversity, many of the PTs tended to downplay or ignore student diversity and "lump" students with other than white European ancestry as "other," at least initially. Some PTs overestimated the proportion of African American students, referred only to African American and white students (despite substantial Hispanic minorities at both schools), or referred to students of other than white European ancestry as black. In other words, many of the new teachers reduced diversity to difference, specifically "different from me." At least in the beginning of their experiences at Royalton and Charter School, they kept their focus on themselves. Ken and Lynn continued to do so, while Mark and Jaclyn moved on and reached out to connect with their students.

3

They Say, They Keep Telling Us

Schools communicate messages about "who we are," "how we do things here," and the like. While there are numerous similarities across most schools, there are important differences as well. Newcomers' survival and success depend to a considerable extent on "listening" for the school's messages and dealing with them in constructive ways. That is not always easy to do. Messages may be subtle or indirect. There might be mixed messages. Some messages might impede or contradict good practice. Moreover, messages to newcomers about "how we do things here," "how to survive," or "how to get along here" are not necessarily received, and even if they are received, they are not always interpreted as intended by the senders. Importantly, prospective and new teachers differ both in the number and nature of messages they report receiving and how they interpret and act on them. From the examples provided here, one can gain some idea of what to expect in similar situations and begin to anticipate ways of dealing with the messages that constitute "institutional press."

In this chapter, the focus is on the messages about students and teaching that you are likely to encounter in and around urban schools, including messages about the schools themselves, and more or less constructive ways of dealing with these messages as a prospective or newer teacher. Examples are drawn from other kinds of schools as well in order to illustrate differences in messages and ways they are communicated and negotiated. Most of these examples come from interviews and on-site observations, as well as informal conversations with teachers and other school personnel. For example, an elementary student-teacher in a 4th-grade classroom in a largely rural school district, who was enthusiastic about teaching "hands-on" science, found a class set of worksheets provided with the school's science textbook on her desk the morning she was to teach her first science lesson. The message was clear: She was expected to use the textbook and the accompanying worksheets (Abell & Roth, 1994).

Imagine that you are a prospective teacher who has been at your city school Field Experience site for 2 to 3 months. Now you are looking toward student-teaching there after winter break. You've come to know your way around the building and grounds and maybe the surrounding area. You've also come to know school personnel, especially the teacher who will be your co-op, and at least some of your students. Perhaps you've even been able to teach part or all of a class as well as observe several different teachers. Although you are not yet an insider, you're feeling like less of an outsider. The school seems familiar, if not yet comfortable. Some of your initial concerns have been validated. Others have not turned out to be as serious as you anticipated. How has your experience at a school that is different from your own elementary or secondary school experience shaped or reshaped your beliefs and practice with regard to student difference and diversity and to teaching there?

"MESSAGES" AS A WAY OF INFLUENCING NEW TEACHERS

A major way that schools and other settings exert influence is through the messages they send. Messages can be communicated personally, as in a cooperating teacher giving advice or another teacher telling stories in the teachers' lounge. Messages also can be embedded in bureaucracy, as in rules and regulations, prevailing norms, or simply "how we do things here." Finally, messages can be carried by technical means such as the school schedule, the nature and availability of facilities and materials, or mandated exams.

Jaclyn, a prospective social studies teacher at Royalton High School, described messages being communicated to newcomers like herself and to students by "inspirational posters" on the school's walls "that nobody really looks at"; teachers "in the hallways in between classes telling kids to go to class, go to class, go to class"; and the morning announcement that counts down the minutes students have left to get to class. Teachers were a major source of messages that Jaclyn received. "I observe them or talk to them and see [pause] um, sort of how it works here and what I should be doing when I come in. . . . I do see things like the Regents [state exams] being pressured."

Another example of messages being communicated by stories is provided by Chris, a new physical education teacher in a rural school district. She described hearing

> stories from students and teachers about teachers who were released the year before. The art teacher, last year, shaved his head and let the kids paint on it. It was something a little too radical for a small town like this, and so he was out the next year. (quoted in Schempp, Sparkes, & Templin, 1993, p. 463).

In her school, messages about appropriate or expected teacher appearance, attitudes, and behavior were more common than messages about teaching.

An example of an indirect message, communicated by technical means, concerns the shortage of textbooks and other instructional materials at Royalton High School. English and social studies teachers, for example, only had one class set of textbooks (or any other books) for each subject they taught. That meant that students could not take books home for homework or to study for an exam. A few books might be available during a student's study hall if some students in the class using them that period were absent that day. Recall Amanda's description of the conditions at Royalton compared to her own high school (see Chapter 2).

Regarding her situation at Royalton High School, Amanda said, "When I think about how much time I'm going to have to plan into lesson plans for just physically reading . . . it lessens what you can do and how many activities you can do with the students and all that." In other words, both teaching and learning suffer from the lack of sufficient materials. Opportunity to learn is diminished.

Amanda repeated the "making do" message at Royalton and the feeling on the part of some students as well as teachers "that what they were getting was second rate, that they didn't have the resources, they didn't have the best teachers [or students]." There was too much acceptance for Amanda, "a very different mentality" from what she was accustomed to. As will be shown, she worked hard, with some success, not to give in to such messages.

For most of the prospective teachers assigned to Charter School or Royalton High School, their first encounter with the school occurred before they ever entered the building, as described in the previous chapter. This virtual encounter came through local and other media portrayals of urban or city schools and more general accounts in readings for university classes. The media portrayals were largely negative, highlighting violence (fights among students sometimes injuring adults trying to intervene), low test scores, or high dropout rates. Class readings more often stressed problems or challenges compared to suburban schools. The overall message was that teaching at Charter School, and especially Royalton, would be difficult. This message was amplified by friends, families, and others who echoed the negative media images to PTs once their placement at an urban school was known.

When they were on-site for their Field Experience practicum during the fall semester, prospective teachers encountered mixed messages from teachers and other school personnel about Royalton and its students as well as continuing, most often negative, messages from external sources.

Messages sent and received can change over time, in specifics, or in mix and emphasis. Regardless of the nature and extent of any change, the messages continue. Prospective and newer as well as experienced teachers, however, may come to tune out some of them while attending to others. Over time, for example, most prospective teachers became quite defensive about Royalton High School and its students, and they reported trying to counter, if not correct, external misconceptions. Fortunately for dealing constructively with difference and diversity, most PTs rejected the crudely negative internal messages they reported about "these students" and distanced themselves from the teachers who voiced them. Not surprisingly, relatively few such negative messages surfaced during informal interviews or conversations with teachers and other school personnel.

At Charter School, prospective teachers reported very few "messages," perhaps because of the consistency promoted by structured academic and behavioral programs. Messages are less obvious when there is little difference of opinion or practice. Although only seven messages were reported by the four Charter School PTs, five were negative. Negative messages concerned parents, administration, and other teachers, but not students or the school as a whole.

Overall, more than three times as many negative messages as constructive or neutral ones were reported by prospective teachers at both schools. This is not surprising, since negative messages are more likely to be vividly conveyed and remembered than positive or neutral ones. Moreover, there probably are more negative messages to begin with, just as "news" sources report muggings, ignoring all the people who were not mugged. Prospective teachers who reported the most negative messages were not necessarily the most negative themselves. In fact, they were among the more successful PTs in constructively engaging student difference and diversity (and those who reported the most messages overall). So, negative messages are not necessarily destructive.

The kinds of messages that the largest number of prospective teachers (at Royalton unless otherwise noted) reported are as follows:

- General negativism about urban schools and students (from various, largely external sources) (69% of PTs, 92% at Royalton)
- Different teacher groups, especially negative ones (75%)
- Royalton High School as a good school despite current problems and day-to-day differences among staff members (58%)
- Difference and diversity among students (58%)
- Control or discipline (50%)
- Range of student skills, motivation, behavior (33%)

- Connecting with students and creating engaging lessons (33%)
- Low academic expectations for students (33%)

Relatively few PTs reported more specific messages about teaching the students in their classes. Perhaps advice and feedback on teaching were seen as what cooperating teachers and university supervisors do rather than as messages.

Each of these clusters of messages is illustrated below, along with the ways that prospective teachers have dealt with them. Available examples from other urban schools also are included. Then, the nature and apparent effects of different ways of responding are considered.

GENERAL NEGATIVISM FROM EXTERNAL SOURCES

These messages formed a backdrop to the more specific messages that prospective teachers encountered within their school site. Most often, the messages came from friends, family, coworkers at part-time jobs, teachers at other schools, and the media. It seemed that the personally delivered messages often echoed and sometimes elaborated media accounts, which themselves may have exaggerated events. For example, a fight between two girls at Royalton High School in the early fall of 2004, at least one of whom had a knifelike weapon, seriously injured a teacher who tried to intervene while increasing numbers of students looked on until school security arrived and stopped the fight. This fight near the beginning of the school year was the first of several at Royalton High School that year and the next, earning the school considerable notoriety in the local television and print media. Although nasty and in no way to be condoned, the fights did not involve very many students, except as onlookers. Students we spoke with said that they felt safe at the school, that there was no safety problem as long as you stayed out of the rivalries and the fights that resulted.

According to Kaitlyn, a prospective English teacher, "everyone was saying 'it's such a horrible school,' 'look it's on the [TV] news'." She described trying to defend Royalton, telling the naysayers, "you don't understand. It's not the school, it's just, you know, a couple of kids." Renee, a prospective social studies teacher, concurred, saying, "I don't really feel threatened or unsafe. . . . I'm just very comfortable." Cora, a prospective science teacher, echoed Renee, saying:

I mean, it is just a school like any other. I mean, it's got its problems. I mean, I am not afraid to walk the halls, I am not afraid to sit in class-

rooms, I am not afraid to interact with the students. It was a lot
different from the initial impression I had when I was walking in.

Half of the prospective teachers at Royalton indicated that they had heard
the teacher-conveyed message that "5–10% of the students are challenging behaviorally while the rest are fine; most Royalton High School students are good kids."

That teachers at suburban schools (the prospective teachers' home
schools and/or second student-teaching sites) and two college instructors
in education were among those communicating negative messages about
city schools was particularly disturbing, as well as indicative of how widespread such messages have become. You don't expect newspapers or television to report on the ordinary, peaceful school days or the banks that were
not robbed. Although you might expect teachers to engage in gossip as
much as other occupational groups do, the credibility they carry about
things to do with schooling makes their negativism about urban schools
potentially more destructive than that of, say, dentists.

One of the accounts about a college instructor's negativism was volunteered by Mark, a prospective social studies teacher, who described his
sister's experience at a local college where she is a freshman education
major. He told me that an instructor there said that "at [college], we'll never
send you to a violent school like [Royalton High School]." His sister
responded,

> "My brother's there now," and the instructor just quieted down and
> was, like, "oh, uh, how does he like it there?" And she's [Mark's sister],
> like, "actually, he likes it a lot." And it's just that, you know, I can see,
> just from hearing that, that made me mad. . . . I'm like, "Has that
> teacher been there?" I doubt it, you know, and seen what it's like? . . .
> [T]hat made me really angry.

Mark went on to say, "I picked up on, you know, the pride in that school
[Royalton], and I think that it is . . . a really good school, and there is a lot
of potential there."

Beyond the violence of student fights, the negative messages about city
schools refer to problems of dealing with students who are poor and non-
white, such as their being unmotivated, uncooperative, and/or unprepared
in school. Note that these are problems of adults—teachers, administrators,
and other school personnel—most of whom are white and middle-class.
Negative messages from external sources rarely take a student perspective.

The point of relaying this general negativism about city schools from
external sources is twofold: it provides a continuing background to the more

specific messages one receives at a particular school site; and negativism is difficult to bracket or block out so that it doesn't bias interpretation of direct experiences at the school. Having received multiple negative messages about city schools, it is hard to escape becoming predisposed to expecting "trouble" of one sort or another without having had prior experiences that lead you to be more positive or to just "wait and see." Several of the prospective teachers at Royalton High School talked about trying to keep an open mind, to go in without expectations or with a clean slate. Renee, for example, described trying not to go in with expectations, to "just take it with an open mind." For those PTs who did go in with an "open mind" to see for themselves, the effort appears to have been rewarded.

MIXED MESSAGES

A key aspect of the messages prospective teachers reported receiving, especially at Royalton High School, was that they differed, and sometimes messages contradicted each other. While mixed, even contradictory, messages can be confusing and anxiety-generating, they also can provide options or leeway for prospective teachers. The kind of message reported by the largest number of PTs after the general negativism just described (11 of 12), was about different teacher groups, characterized as the negative teachers and the others (9 of 12). The large majority of PTs who described different messages from different teacher groups rejected or tried to distance themselves from the negative messages and teachers. Knowing what kinds of teacher groups and negative messages you might encounter during Field Experience and Student-Teaching can help you recognize them as rather common, unfortunately, and consider how to deal with them.

Different Teacher Groups: The Negative Teachers

Negative messages target administration at both school and district levels, students, parents, and sometimes other teachers (those whose approach to discipline or instruction differs from the complainant's). At Royalton, teachers emphasized differences between newer or younger teachers and those who had been at the school for a long time (a few for more than 30 years). The old hands presented themselves as more likely to enforce school rules and maintain high academic standards. They also were more likely to refer to a family atmosphere at Royalton High School. Overall, the prospective teachers did not make similar distinctions. Their concern was with teacher negativism as reflected in denigrating students and expressing low expectations for student learning and futures. These negative teachers (who appeared to be a vocal minority) tend to congregate in the faculty lounge, a workroom, or a table in the faculty cafeteria and share their negativism (e.g., about students' abilities, behavior, and futures) not only with one another but also with prospective teachers, newer teachers, and whoever else will listen. Some share their stories with sad, sideways headshaking, others with more enthusiasm.

Renee, a prospective social studies teacher, described "two separate tables of teachers" in the faculty cafeteria that she distinguished as "very, um, reflecting of the environment in the school." You could "kinda see the divide among the teachers that just complain and complain and complain and [say], 'this is awful, this is awful' versus the other teachers that are just, 'hey, it's lunch. Let's eat lunch and talk,' you know." Renee sat at what she called "the fun table." Later, in the interview, when asked about "dominant messages . . . regarding differences and diversity," Renee responded at length:

> I think there's two camps. . . . [T]here's one that is definitely very, don't wanna say racist, but I, I guess would say more judgmental, you know. You hear those comments that "they're [the students] animals," that they're, you know, they're this, they're that. And that's definitely not what you like to surround yourself with [laughs]. But then I think that there are the teachers that say, "No, they're not. They're just like you and I. They just don't have the opportunities that we had. . . . [T]hey are the same as us, and we have to give them the chance to go through what we had, the opportunities," but, you know, then the other teachers [say], "Well, that'll never happen. Look at where they're coming from." They're just, I think there's that, like, quickness to judge. And sometimes even I felt there was this idea that, they're, like, babies, that they need to be treated just like they're incapable of their own thoughts and their own ideas, that if we baby them and baby them and baby them and treat them that way that maybe that will change things, but I think it should be the exact opposite where you should give them their freedom and let them think and use their minds and try to see how it works that way. So, but there's definitely a big division between the just judging them, like, straight off, so, "He shouldn't be here, she shouldn't be here. She's a horrible person, you know, that person shouldn't be here," versus "Well, maybe we're doing something wrong, and we should be doing something else for this student to keep her in school, you know."

Cora, a prospective science teacher, talked about learning from negative teacher examples:

> Like, um, the whole not knowing your students, the "they're hoodlums, they're this, they're that," like all the generalizations I personally don't think are correct. So, hearing that from [some of] the other teachers just makes me more determined not to ever be that way, so I guess that's been good, like, it's, like, a non-example, you know.

She also referred to messages about the low to negative prognoses regarding students' futures, which overlap with messages specifically about low academic expectations considered in the next section:

> even administration, even in the school itself, there are just, there are certain expectations for the students, like, "wow, these students really aren't gonna do well anyway, so why, you know, freak out about it." . . . I guess I kinda get the same feeling from, like, City Hall and stuff, like, they just expect that these kids are either just gonna drop out or get minimum wage jobs, so why bother, which is pretty sad.

Kate, also a prospective science teacher, said, "I started separating myself from it [teacher negativism] a lot too because I couldn't take it. . . . I think it was the same people and the same complaints day after day." One way Kate separated herself was by eating lunch in her classroom while her cooperating teacher ate his lunch with other negative teachers.

Amanda, a prospective English teacher, also commented on teacher negativism at lunch:

> I think some people . . . kind of feel like glorified babysitters, and they act like it, and they don't think these kids have futures, and I think that just sort of came across in how they acted, and so I didn't find, like, lunch to be a positive experience.

Amanda also noted that:

> a lot of people were really free [with] advice. It wasn't always positive advice, but a lot of people were really willing to, like, to make suggestions. You just have to find the right people and kind of block out the negative voices.

And Malcolm, a prospective social studies teacher, talked about Room 110, a teachers' lounge and workroom with the main copy machine for teacher use, as a gathering place for negative teachers, and then of his more positive experience with his cooperating teacher. Later, he talked about finding refuge in his classroom and with colleagues in his department:

> just the comments, like it was a place that I didn't ever want to walk into; it was a place that was really disgusting, the comments you heard coming out of people's mouths about students, about education and how crappy their jobs are, sorry for my foul language, um, you know, how bad things were, and how bad the students were and how it was so bad, and it was just like "I'm just going to make my photocopies and get out of here," you know, no meaningful discussions. Those were so few and far between. I mean, there were some teachers that, don't get me wrong, I made some, I found some really great teachers, people that I really enjoy their company including Mr. [his co-op], and who wanted to talk about things, who wanted to discuss things, who wanted to talk about teaching, or . . . something that we both enjoyed, it was something that was important to us, . . . a book, something other than "kids are just horrible creatures." . . . I mean, I don't know if you've heard that from other people, but that was one of the things, you didn't like hanging out down there. . . .
>
> I never went down to the lunchroom. I was the hermit up on the third floor, so I wasn't down in the lunchroom too much, but I'm sure it was the same. It was a very big part of the mentality there, so I mean, that gets in the way obviously, um, [sighs] I don't know what else. . . . I didn't get that sense of community at all. I got a very limited sense of that, I got a factional sense, like different factions in the school, we got this faction, we got the old guard, the new guard, but then within that there's always other breakdowns between this group of people, um, I didn't see like a lot of cross-curricular type of discussion. . . . [T]hat's another thing, there was nothing like "this is positive, let's work with this." It was always "this is negative let's fix it." Well, why not work with some of the positive aspects. . . .

Kate, Amanda, and Renee also talked about keeping to themselves to avoid teacher negativism and/or seeking out more positive teachers for ideas and support. Others, including Ken, Lynn, and Ethan, seemed to accept and take on or adopt the negativism that they heard from their co-ops and from other teachers.

Low Academic Expectations

Low academic expectations for students is the third of the clusters of negative messages reported by Royalton PTs (33%). In contrast, while Charter

School PTs referred to students having problems with an academic task, needing more time or help, they did not express or report low expectations. Instead, they communicated a matter-of-fact, "can do" expectation that students would learn if provided with the needed support. At Royalton, Renee, a prospective social studies teacher, told us, "teachers have such low expectations of them [students], and they [the students] kinda play into that." Later in the interview, she said, "I think they're capable of so much, but they're just stuck in this system that pushes them down and doesn't try to lift them, just keeps pushing them down." Her co-op, she related, urged her to just cover the basic information that students needed to know, presumably for exams, and move on, "you know, give 'em some notes or give them the book and 10 questions to answer, like guided reading kinda stuff." She continued:

> The few times that I would bring in my own reading or, you know, another thing for them to look at, he [her co-op] would say, "Oh, this is too hard. They can't do this. Let them use the textbook." Or "no, no, no, they need to be using the textbook. It really breaks it down for them." . . . [I]t got to the point where I just kinda accepted defeat.

Whereas Renee felt worn down by her co-op, Kate, a science PT (see Chapter 2), eventually wore down her co-op and successfully resisted his preoccupation with classroom management, his low expectations for students, and his advice to stick with worksheets and note-giving and not to "push them to think too hard." And Amanda, an English PT who noted negative messages from other teachers, described her co-op as very positive and persistent, with high expectations for students. Recall Amanda saying, "You just have to find the right person and kind of block out the negative voices." Overall, the prospective teachers who reported messages about low academic expectations for students did not appear to buy into them.

MORE CONSTRUCTIVE MESSAGES

On the more constructive or hopeful side, messages about Royalton as a good school going through hard times (mentioned by 58% of the prospective teachers) also include messages such as "the building has a family atmosphere" and "the faculty cares about the school and student success despite day-to-day differences." These messages can be seen as countering, to some extent, the previously described negative ones. The "Royalton as a good school" message was taken up by social studies and English PTs but not science PTs. For two female PTs, one English and one social studies, this message seemed to offer reassurance and encouragement, something to hang on to in turbulent times.

Kaitlyn, a prospective English teacher, described the effort to sustain a "family atmosphere" as providing needed support to both students and teachers. In her words:

> I honestly think it is very much a family of both student and teacher. They connect well 'cause in that environment [likely referring to poverty, violence, and instability] the teacher really has to reach out and make it a family, in the classroom or on a whole, 'cause fighting or keeping that barrier between the two is just a downward battle. . . . [M]aybe it was even more of a family then [several years ago, prior to the district's school choice program] because you were neighborhood kids, you grew up together, and you kind of had your school.
>
> The teachers and, um, especially the principal are very into keeping it a family atmosphere, that you have that support system, that you know the teachers are there, or the staff is there to help you, and hopefully through that type of a bond it will help the students continue through. . . . [T]here are definitely squabbles within the school, tension between certain students and certain teachers, or teachers on teachers . . . teacher and administration, students and administration, but they're always working towards something that's better for the school, that higher good, so they're there for each other and they're around, and you always know when needed you have a person to go to and talk about it.

Kaitlyn appeared to have used the support system she found at Royalton, both to buoy her spirits against giving up or giving in to pessimism and to provide practical suggestions.

> The comment of "it's a good school and they're good kids" is very, very common. [It's] hard to go throughout your day without hearing such a phrase, and it's a phrase I use now all the time, um, 'cause the stereotype of the school is "it's inner-city, they're gang, they're horrible kids, they swear, they're violent, they don't want to learn, they don't want to be there," just, you know, "get rid of them," and it's really, it's a good school with a good staff with good kids for the most part. . . . [Y]ou just have to figure out how to reach them and how to work your lesson plans around them.

Initially, at cohort meetings during the fall semester Field Experience, Jaclyn, a prospective social studies teacher, voiced her discomfort (apparently shared by a few other PTs who tended not to speak up in public settings) about being in the minority as a white person at Royalton. She was won over, however, by her experience there. About family atmosphere, she told me after quite successfully completing her student-teaching at Royalton:

> They really sell that to you the minute you walk in the door, that it's a big family, and I really felt that it was. I saw that it was, I heard that it was, and I think that's very true. So, even though they have their problems, they do pull together, and you can see that in the school. . . . I think that the teachers there feel that if they form a bond together and if they hold strong, that their students will see that and almost, um, conform to it in a way and stick together themselves as having pride in their school and, um, just making positive things happen rather than looking at the negative things.

Jaclyn went on to say that she sees a family atmosphere at Royalton "more than I saw it in my high school growing up, more than I see it at my second placement." And, importantly, she came to feel that she was part of it, rather than continuing to feel like an outsider.

Mark, also a prospective social studies teacher, referred to messages from students, his cooperating teacher, and other teachers about pride in the school, about Royalton being "a really good school, and there is a lot of potential there." He mentioned his co-op and colleagues with whom his co-op interacts as giving off "a sense of, you know, 'we really care'." According to Mark, they don't think of it as just a job. They arrive early and leave late, take initiative, and take pride in their work and the school. Mark said, "that actually made an impact on me, like, that they're there to do things. . . . [T]hey're there to teach," not simply to get through the day. Like Jaclyn, Mark felt an early apprehension about Royalton, given his experience at a predominantly white, suburban high school. It was mitigated, however, by his experience with enthusiastic teachers, and he too maintained an academic emphasis in his teaching.

Creating Engaging Lessons

The second cluster of positive or constructive messages is the only instructionally oriented one—about connecting with students and creating engaging lessons (33%, all 2nd-year PTs). While several 1st-year PTs said that connecting with students in positive ways was one of their major goals or concerns, they did not present it as a message. Similarly, several 1st-year

PTs commented that creating engaging lessons decreases problems and increases student success, but did not necessarily present the claim as a message. Mark, for example, said that "bad teachers" make discipline a top priority instead of teaching, but that "if you concentrate on teaching, the discipline will kind of come. . . . [F]rom what I observed, I saw that a lot." He also mentioned getting this message from university instructors.

During year two, Cora, Ethan, and Kaitlyn reported messages about active learning working well with Royalton students, about trying to reach students with different methods and activities, and about how "you always want energy going into the classroom, you always want to be there to teach." To get students to care, show them you care, "starting off with their name . . . always finding something positive" (Kaitlyn). Jaclyn spoke at some length about this message and acting on it, beginning with "It's the most important thing to do with the students if you plan on being successful. You had to connect with them. If you didn't, you lost them, there's just nothing."

N/EITHER CONSTRUCTIVE N/OR NEGATIVE MESSAGES

A third set of messages reported by at least one-third of the prospective teachers at Royalton High School cannot be characterized as either constructive or negative; in a sense, they are both.

Difference and Diversity

Messages about student difference or diversity (58%) included comments about the demographic mix of students at the school and about the majority of students getting along well. It was noted that both closer friendships and fights occurred within racial/ethnic and gender groups, and that turf rivalries and "he said, she said" tensions outweighed group identities as sources of problems. The overall message seemed to be that difference and diversity were not "a big deal" at Royalton High School.

Diversity was embraced with what one prospective teacher called a "very Christian overtone," referring to the large Christmas tree in the school's lobby. The following year (2005), another prospective teacher referred to the Christmas decorations as "a little over the top." She didn't think "you should just shove it in everybody's face like that," apparently referring to the school's small Muslim minority. I, too, was surprised by the Christmas tree, but heard no objections other than from these two prospective teachers. In fact, a third prospective teacher commented, "we have all of these Christmas decorations up right now. . . . So I guess in terms of

religious diversity, we are decorated for Christmas. . . . I think it's festive."
Later in the same interview, she noted that "during Ramadan during lunch
[Muslim] students can go up to the library so they wouldn't have to sit and
be around food and other people eating. . . . I never heard of that, probably because I went to a suburban school, and I thought that was very
thoughtful and very sensitive." These three prospective teachers' comments
reflect different degrees of perspective-taking and empathy for others in
their interpretation of messages received, from the third PT whose comments are both observant and self-centered to the second who saw the
decorations as an imposition. In between, the first PT commented disap-
provingly on the apparent contradiction between messages embracing
diversity and celebrating Christmas.

Another message about difference and diversity concerned teacher
responses to any negative student comments about another group, such
as gays or non-Christian holidays or racial slurs. The clear message that
prospective teachers noted was that such disparaging comments are off-
limits at Royalton High School.

Difference and diversity were "a big deal," at least initially, for several of the Royalton PTs. Those who mentioned student race or ethnicity
tended to substantially overestimate the number of African American students and underestimate the number of white students. A few did not
mention or distinguish Hispanic students, apparently categorizing students
who were not visibly European or observant Middle Eastern Muslim
as black. Teachers tended to describe Royalton students as mostly from
working-class or poor homes, implying that socioeconomic status overrode
race/ethnicity/culture. Kaitlyn echoed this view, saying that Royalton students aren't diverse except "when it's in the classroom about ability. . . .
[N]ot too much elsewhere. . . . [I]t looks diverse on the surface, but not
really" because they "come from the same neighborhoods, ride the same
buses, [have] similar experiences."

It is possible that teachers and other school personnel believed that
low socioeconomic status made a bigger difference in Royalton (and Charter School) students' lives than did their race, ethnicity, or culture. It also
is possible that they were more comfortable talking about poverty and/or
did not want to appear racist. Pollock (2004), for example, describes the
adults at a diverse California public high school as "colormute," indicating their reluctance to talk directly about race. Another possibility is that
many Royalton adults saw racial/ethnic/cultural diversity as divisive, or
potentially so, and preferred to stress unity or "family." The message that
student difference and diversity was not "a big deal" at Royalton may well
have encouraged some new teachers to downplay it.

Discipline

Control or discipline messages (50% of prospective teachers) included "be tough," have a "firm presence," and just give notes and worksheets because control is easier with these than with activities. Interestingly, half of the PTs reporting these messages were among the more successful ones, and half were among the least successful. None seemed to reject these messages altogether, but PTs differed in terms of which ones they accepted and how they interpreted them, as will be shown in the sections and chapters that follow.

These are common messages in urban schools. For example, a new teacher advised not "to let details of her personal life seep into lessons" instead talked about her own family's move from Bangladesh to the United States in order to connect with her middle school students during their study of immigration. When another new teacher at the same school tried to follow advice and be "very strict," he found that "it just falls flat." When he started playing basketball with some of his students, relationships improved (Gootman, 2007).

Varying Student Abilities

Messages about student variation in skills, motivation, and behavior (33% of PTs) included the regularly heard message that "5 to 10% of the students are challenging behaviorally; most are good kids." Quite a few of these messages concerned student apathy and low self-expectations. For example, referring to student apathy, Kate noted that her "kids have it rough" insofar as a difficult environment encourages them not to care about school. Amanda told me that too many of her students have low self-expectations, telling her that they "just can't do it." Recall from Chapter 2 that Amanda described her major challenge at Royalton as the students who feel "'I just can't do it, I'm not smart enough' or 'It doesn't matter' . . . 'I just need to get by'." "So," she said, "I think making it matter to them is probably, like, the first goal." Kaitlyn reported similar messages from students retaking an English exam. "They aren't dumb!" she said, "They think they are, but they're not." She also said that the students should have had the help they needed sooner, "before it got to this point."

Like the message about control or discipline, messages about student differences in skills, motivation, and behavior are not unlike messages heard in other schools, except perhaps in degree. That is, control is more important because more students are disruptive, and more students have low skill levels and self-confidence.

EMERGING AND DIVERGING RESPONSE PATHS

As has been indicated in presenting the messages reported by PTs at Royalton High School, they did not report the same messages or the same number of messages. Apart from individual differences in memory and willingness to talk with an interviewer at length, the variation in the number and nature of messages reported seems to be related to who your cooperating teacher was, where you spent your time during lunch and preparation periods, and how receptive you were to teacher gossip, venting, and war stories.

Beyond receiving messages about this school, these students, and teaching here, how and why PTs responded or interpreted and acted on (or chose to ignore) one or another message also appears to be linked to their biographies, that is, to what they brought to the school setting and their role as prospective teachers. Although biography is an important influence on prospective and new teachers, it is not determining. We have choices and are likely to recognize more options and make better decisions when we are aware of what's happening. That awareness can be heightened by learning from the experiences of others as well as by careful observation and reflection.

Prospective and newer teachers have less freedom of action than experienced teachers. Prospective teachers want good grades and reference letters that will help them obtain teaching jobs. Newer teachers want acceptance, support, and contract renewal or tenure. This usually entails "fitting in" and "not making waves" as well as working hard and smart enough to establish one's reputation as a successful teacher. It does not mean being ingratiating or invisible. Most schools, like Royalton, encompass teacher subcultures that enable prospective and newer teachers to fit in somewhere. And persistent, politically savvy prospective and newer teachers can negotiate or create space for doing some things differently within their own classrooms.

Some suggestion of the prospective teachers' different response paths has already been offered. Here, those emerging paths are more fully drawn. I call them:

- Knee-deep in negativity
- Out of the loop
- Avoiding or actively rejecting negativism
- Selectively accepting/adopting constructive notions

Knee-Deep in Negativity

"Knee-deep in negativity" clearly is not a constructive response. It tends toward a kind of lamenting, woe-is-me-ism as one accepts the seeming inevitability of a difficult situation over which one presumably has no influence. Given this perception, there is little or nothing that the PT sees her- or himself able to do but try to survive, to stick it out and then move on. Lynn, a prospective science teacher, seems to have followed this path. She noted substantial academic and what she called "cultural" differences between Royalton High School and its students and her own mostly white, affluent, suburban high school. She wasn't personally aware of poverty before, she said, and "I had never heard good things about city schools." Her cooperating teacher was a strong disciplinarian whom she described as "very much [a] lecture, worksheet, take notes type of person." Lynn continued, "and he has good reason for it as a way to reach different types of people with the lectures and the notes and, um, to kind of maintain some sort of structure." Although she said that she was looking forward to using visuals and demonstrations, and that she wasn't sure how to establish classroom management since she didn't have "a big bellowy voice" like her co-op, Lynn presented herself as "just trying to get along. . . . I just tried to blend in and be friendly," especially with her co-op and his colleagues.

Unfortunately, Lynn's cooperating teacher was among the most negative teachers at Royalton. He was especially critical of the school and district administration, often talking in terms of complaints and union grievances. Among the critical messages Lynn reported, almost all from her co-op, was that disruptive student behavior continued because the rules weren't being enforced by other teachers or administrators.

> I keep hearing, you know, there is no penalty for having a cell phone, for wearing a hoodie, for all of these things that they aren't supposed to do, and even if you get detention and you don't show up, it doesn't matter. Nothing happens to you. . . . [A]nd there are so many teachers that let this slide that, um, things just keep happening.

Her cooperating teacher presumably was one of the few who tried to enforce the rules.

Lynn shared her belief that "as a student-teacher, I just have to follow along and hear what my CT says and what he thinks." Asked whether she thought her co-op and his opinions influenced her, Lynn responded:

> Oh, sure, it probably did, because I spent so much time with him and his friends that I think it had to, but I think in a lot of cases he had good points, and he wasn't just, like, being vindictive. But, um, sometimes I think he also went over the top. Like, administration would do one little thing and they would be in an uproar, like "oh, I don't like this. I don't like this." You can just, like, "oh, we might have to talk to the union about this."

Although she recognized that sometimes these negative messages went "over the top," Lynn felt obligated to go along and, in the process, she seemed to adopt some of the other teachers' negativity about Royalton High School and their low expectations for Royalton students.

Although Lynn's response to the messages she received appears more like passivity and dependence on her cooperating teacher than inherent negativity, she did seem predisposed to negative messages about urban schools. Yet, one wonders how her experience at Royalton might have differed if her co-op was more upbeat about the school and held higher expectations for the students.

A variant of "knee-deep in negativity" not only laments but also seems to be trying to shock the listener as s/he relates the negative messages about how bad things are. Where Lynn "goes along" with her cooperating teacher's largely negative messages, Ethan is better described as "passing on" the largely negative messages he encounters from various teachers and other school personnel. Ethan, a prospective English teacher, seemed to enjoy this path. Despite expressing disapproval of such negativity, he appeared to do much more to witness and convey than resist or combat it. For example, in our first interview, Ethan began by talking about some teachers who "tend to complain a lot . . . [who] constantly talk about the union and the superintendent and how that's not fair anymore. It's, it's a bit stressful." He continued:

> I am constantly around a certain group of teachers, and they talk about it. From what I understand, it is a conversation that is easy to get roped into, so other teachers join in. Like, I do know that I have spoken with other teachers about these issues, and they say, "oh, well, you know, there are some people who just want to cause trouble and some people here who just want to complain." . . . [T]here are some teachers that complain just way too much. They should probably just accept things as they are and just work.

Ethan also reported hearing negative messages about students, but was not very specific:

> The way some of the teachers talk about the students actually. A lot of the teachers there, and I'm not saying all of them, I'm not saying they're bad people, people need to vent, um, after dealing with these kids I totally understand you need to go some place and blow off some steam, hence the faculty lounge. But, I've seen teachers mistreat students, I've seen them not care enough or pretend not to hear something, you know, it bothers me, and I feel like this is a product of

how teachers view the students. I think that their class, their race, and their geographic location all factor into that as well as the students' attitude obviously.

By our third conversation, Ethan was attributing continuing negative messages to teacher "venting":

> I spent a lot of time in the teachers' lounge. . . . [T]hese teachers did argue a lot, the faculty complained a lot about their students, and there was always gossip, and there was always a rumor, there was always something going on, and a lot of it was just annoying grievances about the school system, and about the new regime and about how things were working and about the good old days, how things were just awesome, and, you know, everything was great. But you knew that they were trying, you always knew that they were venting. You didn't think, "wow, this person's a horrible teacher, he's angry at a student." You just thought, "this man is venting."

Clearly, Ethan seemed to relish relating and interpreting these messages and no longer said that he found them stressful. Nor did he say why he chose to spend so much time in the teachers' lounge or, in contrast to Lynn, report any of these messages as coming from his cooperating teacher.

In part because of how they interpreted and responded to the messages they reported receiving, and the amount of time Ethan apparently spent taking in largely negative messages, Lynn and Ethan were among the less successful PTs at Royalton.

Out of the Loop

"Out of the loop" is neither an inherently constructive or destructive path. It reflects not picking up on and/or reporting the school's "messages"—in contrast to Ethan, who seems to have sought them out. Neither of the two Royalton PTs in this group spoke much in the cohort meetings with their university supervisor-mentor; they seemed passive and/or shy. Both appeared to stay close to home, with their cooperating teachers, at the school site. While Ken's co-op was among the more outspoken negative teachers, Rupert's was among the more constructive teachers, who tended to keep to themselves or mingle with like-minded colleagues. In interviews, both referred to their co-ops numerous times and appeared to be trying to follow their advice, which they apparently did not see as messages.

Being "out of the loop" and trying to follow one's cooperating teacher's advice may not impede short-term survival, but it is a risky strategy over the longer term, even with a very constructive co-op. It is risky because one can too easily become overwhelmed as a new teacher at a new school site without the "protection" or guidance of a cooperating teacher and without experience negotiating the push-pull of various messages, individuals, and groups within a school. Better to have had some experience interpreting and dealing with a school's often mixed messages as a student-teacher aided by the support system of co-op, cohort colleagues (other student-teachers at the site), and a university supervisor-mentor. With some idea of what to expect, available response options, and their likely consequences, new teachers experience much less stress and more confidence in their ability to deal with institutional press. With less stress and more confidence, they have more time and energy to focus on teaching and learning. Moreover, they are better able to make good use of a teacher mentor if one is available because they can at least begin to identify and clarify their questions and consider possible responses. They are neither clueless nor overly dependent.

Importantly, the "out of the loop" response path, like "knee-deep in negativity," appears to be shaped more by the prospective teacher than by the cooperating teacher and the school site. Lynn (knee-deep) and Ken (out of the loop) in science had the same co-op in different years, as did Rupert (out of the loop) and Mark (to be considered later as "selectively accepting/adopting constructive notions") in social studies. Lynn told us that even though she thought that her co-op and his colleagues were "over the top" in their negativity at times, she felt obligated as a student-teacher to try to follow his lead with respect to discipline and instruction with very few modifications. Ken, in contrast, missed the "messages" and saw his co-op as providing good advice, especially feedback, regarding discipline and instruction. Sometimes, in speaking with me, Ken seemed to be parroting things I had heard his co-op say (e.g., criticism of administrators). Although neither was very successful as a student-teacher at Royalton High School, Lynn arguably is likely to negotiate the messages of a new school site more successfully than Ken because she recognized messages as such and decided how to deal with them rather than follow along by default.

Like Rupert, Mark was positively impressed by his co-op and tried to follow his lead. Yet Mark, as has been suggested and will be described shortly, was aware of other messages, especially destructive ones, and purposefully chose to adopt the more constructive ones. From this experience, he seems more likely than Rupert to successfully negotiate the mixed messages of other school sites.

The remaining two paths represent more constructive responses to messages about Royalton High School, its students, and teaching there. The difference between the two is largely one of emphasis, either on rejecting negativism or adopting constructive notions. Malcolm, Kate, and Cora offer the clearest illustrations of avoiding or actively rejecting negative messages, while Jaclyn and Mark provide the clearest illustrations of selectively adopting constructive notions. Amanda, Kaitlyn, and Renee followed a mixed response path that incorporates both avoiding and rejecting some messages and accepting/adopting others.

Avoiding or Actively Rejecting Negativism

Of particular interest here are efforts to resist negative messages about "these students" and "teaching here" because they are most relevant to dealing constructively with difference from mainstream, middle-class, white culture and with diversity. When teachers say, "Well, you know, these kids can't do this, or they can't do that" or " they're never gonna get this" or "this is way over their heads," Malcolm told me, they are referring to mainly working-class and poor students, most of whom are African American or Hispanic. White, middle-class teachers are denigrating students who are different from themselves by communicating low academic expectations. One can resist this by avoiding the sources of such messages as Malcolm, a prospective social studies teacher, did. Recall his self-description as "the hermit up on the third floor." When Malcolm did encounter a negative message, he quietly rejected it. "I would listen, and I would take it in . . . I would smile and say thank you . . . but I wouldn't follow it." He gave an example regarding relationships with students:

> people were always trying to give you that kind of direction [about students], like . . . there were certain teachers that were, like, you know . . . you can treat them like they're human beings, you know, if they want to give you a hug, if they just wanna come up and "hey, how you doing today?" and slap hands, and there were teachers that were completely disgusted, and I use the word *disgusted*, not just *opposed*, they were disgusted by that type of behavior where that's not the role of a teacher, you're not their friend at all, you're not any type of, um, figure that might, um, care about them at all, you know. A handshake in the hallway, how dare you, especially coming from a population of primarily African American kids where, um, a handshake, a handslap, whatever you want to call it, is a sign of respect, it's something, it's nice; if you don't do that, a kid would look at you, like, "what, you're too good to shake my hand?" . . . [some teachers] would say, "don't let students get out of their seats, you've got to take control of the classroom," um, I can honestly say I pretty much ignored everything [like that] that was said to me. I really did.

Malcolm was fortunate to be working with one of the more open, positive, and energetic cooperating teachers at Royalton High School, and he was able to find support for his ideas "at home." These ideas included working on student comprehension of big ideas and issues such as social justice, in part by figuring things out for themselves with his guidance and support. He also "found some really great teachers" whose company and conversation he enjoyed.

Kate, a prospective science teacher, had a different experience. She actively rejected her cooperating teacher's low academic expectations for students and instructional advice to stay with the textbook and simple worksheets. According to her CT, the textbook and worksheets would give students what they needed to pass required science tests and make discipline easier than would more academically and behaviorally challenging group activities, projects, or discussions. Kate rejected these messages and persisted in actively resisting her co-op's pressure to conform to his way of thinking and teaching. Recall (see Chapter 2) that she also persisted in encouraging her students to do the activities that required more than filling in a worksheet. Eventually, as she experienced successes with alternative ways of relating to students and teaching, including having students figure things out or think critically, he backed off a bit. In addition to actively rejecting the negativism of her co-op, Kate also avoided his similarly negative colleagues, including the science teacher next door who was Ken's and then Lynn's cooperating teacher, in part by eating lunch in her classroom while her co-op and his friends ate in the faculty cafeteria or lounge. Additionally, Kate sought advice and support from other teachers at Royalton. As she described it, "I did now and then go to a different teacher and say, 'I kind of want to do this, and I don't know exactly how to work it,' and they would help me out."

The negative messages that Cora, also a prospective science teacher, actively rejected had more to do with perceptions of different groups of students than with how she taught. Like Kate, Cora wanted to engage students in activities and critical thinking. Her cooperating teacher was more skeptical than opposed; Cora described her as rather negative and kind of burned out. She referred to her co-op's lamenting that Royalton High School and its students had gone "downhill" and were not what they used to be. There were other teachers, Cora said, who didn't get to know their students and would say "'they're hoodlums, they're this, they're that,' like all the generalizations I personally don't think are correct." These negative messages, Cora said, "sort of reinforce . . . what I want to do." Other negative messages that Cora noted and wanted to avoid included calling on males more than females in science classes. "It's telling the girls that they aren't good at science already [in 9th grade]," she said, and "it happens all the time . . . the girls are ignored a lot." Cora also commented on various messages conveying low expectations for students and that "these kids aren't dumb [spoken loudly]. They know what people are saying about them, so obviously, like, if they keep hearing it, you're just going to get the whole self-fulfilling prophecy thing, which, what good does that do anybody?"

Malcolm, Kate, and Cora avoided and rejected negativism. Malcolm and Kate actively sought out more positive teachers for ideas and support. Kate, however, was in the difficult position of rejecting her co-op's advice and challenging his way of teaching. Her position took considerable strength of character as well as knowledge and skill. All three prospective teachers appeared to enter the school site with a strong sense of how they wanted to teach and what they wanted their students to learn.

Selectively Accepting/Adopting Constructive Notions

Both Jaclyn and Mark attended predominantly white, middle-class, suburban–small-town high schools. They came to Royalton with some apprehensions about city schools, but said that they tried to keep an open mind about the school and its students. For the most part, they put aside the negative messages about urban schools that they encountered to focus on constructive messages about getting to know their students and teaching them (in this case, social studies). Jaclyn gave priority to constructive messages about connecting with students so you can teach them, while Mark emphasized teaching that engages students. They seemed to be approaching the same goal from somewhat different starting points.

Connecting with students in positive ways, Jaclyn told us, was a message that she heard before she got to Royalton, when she arrived, and while she was there:

> It's the most important thing to do with the students if you plan on being successful. You had to connect with them. If you didn't, you lost them, there's just nothing. . . . I tried many different things. With the girls, they would talk about, you know, shopping things or music, and I would try to, you know, get interested and ask them things. With the boys, I, um, I am interested, I really am interested in sports, and they didn't think I was, they didn't think I knew anything that was going on. The Super Bowl was going on. They were just like, "Oh Miss, did you see the Super Bowl last Thursday?" Just trying to, like, trick me, to make sure, um, that they were right. "Oh yeah, it was on Thursday?

That's funny, you know, I thought it was on Sunday!" It was really
funny, and it was a way that I could connect with them, so I felt, I felt
really good about that.

Other examples Jaclyn related were about being at the classroom doorway
between classes and learning students' names as described in Chapter 2.
In these ways, classroom management followed from Jaclyn's connecting
with students and substantive teaching. It was a consequence rather than
a prerequisite.

Mark connected with students through subject matter and involving
more students in classroom activities. He said, "Looking back, I just, I just
realized . . . it's all about relevancy, you know, how you make things relevant. . . . [I]t's not just history, it's the study of people, how people react to
different situations and different events, things like that." He continued:

And in most cases, if you look closely enough, you can find things that
relate to, um, student lives or to relate to current events going on now.
. . . [S]tudents at [Royalton], they were very in tune to current events.
So, they know what's going on, they know what [George W.] Bush is
doing and what they don't like about what Bush is doing. . . . [W]hen
you, like, start with the founding fathers and government and things
like that, how you can . . . "How do you think they react?" "Would you
react differently to, you know, what Bush would do?" And just giving
them a compare and contrast, because they have to understand the
material and then they have to critically think about it. . . . [T]he
students responded to that very well.

Recall Mark saying that, "if you concentrate on teaching, the discipline will
kind of come." His cooperating teacher's advice and his own predisposi-
tions meshed well.

Jaclyn and Mark selectively accepted and adopted constructive messages about teaching Royalton students while distancing themselves from
negative messages and later minimizing them as, for example, coming
from a teacher who was having "a bad day." Both connected with their
students and took academic teaching and learning seriously. Jaclyn elaborated on how she got to know her students, how she would "catch their
attention" and hold them responsible in order to teach global history.
Mark talked more about making U.S. history and government relevant
to students, encouraging active student involvement and critical thinking, while acknowledging that in order to do so, you have to know your
students, "what's really going on" in their lives. Also evident in Jaclyn's
and Mark's conversations was that they worked hard—like Malcolm,

Kate, and Cora—putting considerable time, energy, and thought into their student-teaching.

SO, WHAT'S THE MESSAGE?

First, understand what you are likely to encounter as a new teacher in an urban school, especially the negative messages about urban schools and students that can undermine the confidence and effort of both teachers and students. Then, consider how you might deal with a range of messages in more rather than less constructive ways. Use the examples of the prospective teachers provided here as a guide, not as rules to follow, but as suggestions to be tried out and tested in your own situation.

What might seem like a focus on negative messages here—general negativism from external sources and the negative teacher group—is in part a reflection of what occurs in schools like Royalton and in metropolitan areas throughout the United States. More importantly, it is intended to help teachers recognize the negativism as chronic, not particular to their school, and to move beyond it. It simply is not helpful, except perhaps to boost the status of the conveyor of negativism as someone "in the know" and/ or someone better than those whom s/he is denigrating—or to elicit sympathy for one's presumably awful situation. General negativism from external sources also can be part of an effort to assuage guilt about no longer living or teaching in the city or not sending one's own children to urban public schools.

On re-reading Lois Weiner's *Urban Teaching, The Essentials* (2006), I was struck by the fit between her description of conditions in urban schools and the "messages" that prospective teachers encountered at Royalton High School. For example, Weiner describes herself as "sad to acknowledge" that:

> in more schools than not—everywhere, not just cities—the discussion in the teachers' lounge tends to be negative; positive comments about teaching seem out of place. Unfortunately, especially for new teachers, it's the last place to go for help. . . . In general, this is not a great place for you to spend your time out of the classroom if you want to retain your idealism. . . . Perhaps you'll be able to filter out the negative [if you do frequent the lounge], but don't think that you need to bond in the lounge to be respected by your colleagues. (p. 40)

Minimize your time in the teachers' lounge or wherever the more negative teachers congregate. Hearing the same complaints from the same people, over and over again, is not helpful. Or, see for yourself, and compare how you feel about your students and teaching after spending some time with the negative teachers and then spending the same amount of time on your own (in your classroom or the library, for example) or talking with more constructive teachers. Weiner also advises new teachers to distinguish what they observe first-hand from the stories (or messages) they hear, which may be embellished or untrue.

While minimizing your time with negative teachers and other sources of negative messages is healthy, cutting yourself off from most or all messages probably is not. You will miss constructive messages and support, and may also miss important cautions, for example, about avoiding violations of key cultural norms or policies at the school.

Two positive messages drawn from the examples in this chapter concern reflection and purpose. Regarding reflection, try to step back from difficult situations such as disruptive student behavior in your classroom and consider "what's happening?" rather than personalizing the situation, "taking offense," and reacting in anger. Initially, try to defuse the situation, perhaps with a bit of humor. Then, try to understand the situation from the students' perspective, identify external influences on what happened (for example, something that occurred in the hallway before class or in the community the night before), and resist the temptation to blame the students. Note that offense must be "taken"; it is not simply given. As Weiner (2006), among others, points out, the bureaucratic structure of urban schools, along with their typical policies and practices, encourages authoritarian teaching and custodial treatment of students, neither of which fosters positive teacher-student relationships or meaningful teaching and learning.

With respect to purpose, try to clarify how you want to teach and what you want your students to learn so you can enter your school and classroom with a strong sense of purpose and a clear vision of your identity as a teacher. Malcolm, Kate, and Cora communicate this message, at least implicitly. It is not necessary, and perhaps not even desirable, to have worked out the details in advance; just know where you would like yourself and your students to be headed.

The next three chapters pick up on prospective and newer teachers' initial experiences in urban schools (Chapter 2), the messages they report receiving, and how they dealt with them (Chapter 3) to focus on three different trajectories evident in how they worked with difference and student diversity. Once again, the trajectories illustrate more and less constructive paths in terms of satisfying teacher-student relationships and meaningful student learning—in other words, teacher success. These three paths have broad relevance across preservice teacher education and the experiences of newer and more experienced teachers as documented by the illustrations beyond this project. New teachers may recognize themselves on one or another trajectory and decide to make midcourse corrections.

4

Radical Individualism

This approach to dealing with student difference and diversity that I call radical individualism rejects or attempts to ignore group-linked differences among individuals. Racial/ethnic/cultural and socioeconomic differences as well as differences in gender, religion, sexual orientation, and physical disability are downplayed or avoided because "everyone is different." Only perceived differences in learning or cognitive ability, social behavior, and home language are openly acknowledged. According to this mode of engagement with student difference and diversity, teaching should be individualized to a large extent, because each student is unique. The advantages of this approach for prospective and new teachers are evident in their accounts, which follow. Disadvantages or downsides of radical individualism, especially for students, their communities, and society, are considered in the concluding sections of this chapter.

Radical individualism was more evident among the prospective elementary teachers at Charter School (three of four) than the prospective English, science, and social studies teachers at Royalton High School (one of 12). All three of the Charter School prospective teachers who adopted what I call radical individualism are white, two male and one female: Dante, Kirk, and Sylvia. The Royalton prospective teacher is a black male: Ethan. (One Charter School PT and three Royalton PTs, 25% at each school, did not demonstrate a clear or consistent approach to facing student difference and diversity.)

Of the three prospective elementary teachers at Charter School considered here, Dante appeared most at ease with student difference and diversity, while Kirk experienced what he called "shell shock," and Sylvia seemed awkward with diversity, despite her claims that she was comfortable with people different from herself. Ethan, whose family came to the United States from a Caribbean island, did not like being viewed as African American and repeatedly declared himself an individualist—wanting to be seen as an individual and claiming to see others as individuals. The focus here is on Dante and Kirk and their understandings, experiences, and responses to student difference and diversity. From different starting points, they both came to embrace radical individualism.

DANTE AND KIRK

Dante described himself as naive about the complexity of teaching when he entered the university teacher education program. He was most concerned about how he would be perceived as a male elementary teacher of football player proportions. For example, he wondered how you discipline elementary students without being too loud or intimidating. Dante was one of two male, elementary, prospective teachers in the university program that year, both in the same cohort, at Charter School for Field Experience and their first student-teaching placement, with a male supervisor-mentor. Yet, he tended to speak as if he were the only male elementary PT in the program.

Dante told us, "You know, it's kind of interesting to me because I'm a white male and, you know, it's not very often that a white male will walk into any situation and be considered a minority." In college, Dante started off in exercise science–physical therapy and then switched to communications and public relations before he "came back to teaching," a "feminine field that is, you know, counter, uh, countercultural." Interestingly, Dante did not avoid group-linked characterizations when referring to himself and his situation, as he did when referring to students. I doubt that this divide was apparent to him at the time.

Dante had done some independent research about male elementary teachers as part of the university program, and he talked about it at length. He noted stereotypes about male elementary teachers being pedophiles, homosexuals, or "not smart enough to teach at the secondary level." "And it's just, it's hilarious," he said, because "I am exactly opposite of everything they say, like, I'm supposed to have more feminine characteristics, you know, and basically be a homosexual. And I'm, like, you know, I'm a former Division One college scholarship football player, you know . . . I look more like the gym teacher than I look like an elementary school teacher." In defending himself and his heterosexual masculinity, Dante also seems to be indicating that he shares some of the stereotypes about football players, gym teachers, and gay men as well as male elementary teachers. It was clear to an outsider, although perhaps not to Dante, this was an area of conflict and concern for him.

By the end of his student-teaching experience at Charter School, Dante seemed much less concerned about being a male elementary teacher. He told us that "from being there I learned about a lot of the advantages too of being the only guy around [at least in the area of his 1st-grade classroom on the first floor], little things like . . . I didn't pay for breakfast, I got nice portions at lunch . . . many of the teachers were more than willing to help with a lot of things." He also talked about being a positive male role model for the younger students: "They're used to seeing just the principal being male, and the gym teacher being a male, and the janitor, whereas I come in and show them that it's okay for a male to be [a teacher]." The positives outweigh the negatives, he decided. "I know I have to be aware of how I am perceived, but I know that those situations are things that I can handle."

Moving from a focus on himself to the school, Dante characterized Charter School as similar to the Catholic elementary school he attended through 5th grade except that the latter was almost all white. He had to wear a uniform, as Charter School students do, and "it was very, very disciplined," as is Charter School. Dante also saw the "education level" as similar and much better than the racially and socioeconomically diverse public school he attended in 6th grade, which he described as "like a culture shock" and often chaotic.

Dante described the consistency at Charter School approvingly from the explicit color-coded "card system" for student discipline to teachers "working toward the same goals." He saw the teachers having a "very good rapport" and working well together in part because of team meetings each morning. Because of the longer school day, there is "more one-on-one time" where students get "special reading help" or "help wherever they need help."

Asked about learning to deal constructively with student difference and diversity, Dante talked about adapting curriculum and instruction to different student strengths or abilities.

> Well, one of the things, uh, um, that we talk a lot about is just that you have to reach the students at, that all students are, are smart in different ways [an apparent reference to the concept of multiple intelligences] . . . they do need a different intelligence level or they do need to be taught a different way. All the kids are the same like that because a kid might have a disability and need to be taught a certain way to be successful, but every kid's like that. Every kid needs to be taught the way that they're gonna be the most successful. So if you're not reaching out to them or not differentiating your curriculum, you're gonna miss out on a lot of the students, and I guess you can say their potential for success in your classroom isn't going to be the level that it could.

Dante said that the major thing he learned at Charter School was to take the time to differentiate the curriculum and be flexible enough to take advantage of teachable moments because then students can connect to the subject and remember it better.

Asked about other aspects of student diversity, Dante mentioned cultural differences and linked them with differences in ability and adapting curriculum. He mentioned learning about "where these kids are coming from . . . their culture" and the near-cliché example of students making eye contact with adults as disrespect.

> I guess it's taking what, what you know's going on at home and trying to, to adapt your classroom around that a little bit just to better suit all the students. The way I look at it, it's just, you're gonna have kids with different ability levels, you're gonna have kids with different, different intelligence levels, you're gonna have different kids, kids that come from different cultures. . . . [Y]ou need to change your curriculum for them. You need to adapt to help them because that's why we're here. We're here to get the most out of each of these children. . . . [I]t's gonna be more work for you, but that's what you have to do.

Having taken a special education course emphasizing the inclusion of students with cognitive disabilities in "regular" classrooms, Dante was more amenable to compatible assumptions about "differentiation" at Charter School than he might have been otherwise. Whether Dante was also avoiding talking about other forms of difference among students at Charter School was unclear. The closest he came to talking about "groupness" or group similarities was with respect to teachers when he said, "for as diverse as the student population is, the teaching staff was more of a, of a female, a white female, younger teachers." Dante's awkwardness here suggests some discomfort in talking about others in racial and gender terms. He went on to say that "I almost felt like the message that was being sent [by the teachers] was a common one, that it was a lot of their shared beliefs. . . . I don't think that I was ever around a situation where anything was said, you know, there was anything that was stereotypes made about students." Dante attributed the lack of generalizing or stereotyping of students to their being so diverse that "some would fit the stereotype and some would not even come close to fitting." If he also thought that white teachers might be uncomfortable talking about race and racial differences among students because they might appear racist, and therefore avoided such conversation, he did not say so. Interestingly, all the prospective teachers who adopted Radical Individualism talked about stereotyping as wrong and seemed to see racialized group identifications as racist stereotypes. To avoid racism or being seen as a racist, one avoids racialized group labels such as *black, white,* and *Hispanic.*

Later, during second semester, when asked about any problems he had encountered in working with students whose backgrounds and experiences were different from his own, Dante said that he had not "really faced a problem like that." He attributed his lack of problems to his high school being diverse, and said, "I played a lot of sports that I could have been considered a minority on those teams, and all through college it's been like that." He continued:

> I have always been in diverse situations, so it has never been a problem with me relating to those different students or seeing a way that I could relate. I guess I have a feel for it; I am able to do it. But, I mean, at the same time, I wasn't aware too [that] I had only had small experience with, like, students that English is their second language. So that situation, it could be a little more difficult, but at the same time that's difficult for anyone.

Dante also credited his family experience with helping him relate to a range of students:

> I have a very large family with a lot of different aged kids and ways to reach them. I just have a knack for that, so I don't, I don't think there has ever been a student that no matter how tough they are, so far I mean . . . I don't think I've run across a student that I have looked at like a lost cause. There has been a student that has been more troubling and needed more work, but I was able to figure out a way to relate to him too.

Feeling comfortable applied to working with adults as well. Dante said:

> I can work with just about anyone, and I have a way I, like, I can be dropped anywhere and make friends, so the thing is I'm pretty comfortable, like, I can relate to people on a lot of different levels. . . . I may have met, encountered people who had different beliefs than me, but I did have a respect for them even if I didn't agree with them; it never caused tension or a problem.

In response to a question about changing his ideas or beliefs about difference and diversity, Dante said that "everything has changed so much" since he's been in a classroom rather than just reading about classroom situations. For example, "just working with different students . . . I am just more aware of it [difference and diversity] now than at first. . . . [Y]ou realize that it is an everyday thing that you have to reach the kids on

different levels." Dante distanced himself from those educators who dif-
ferentiated groups of students, saying:

> a lot of people try to focus and make it because this kid has a different
> ethnicity or a student who has a learning disability. I try and not clump
> them. . . . I view a student with a disability or a student with a different
> ethnicity as just another student, that, you know, learns differently or is
> taught better a certain way.

Dante also mentioned that he did not hear teachers stereotyping students, although a few had made negative comments about some parents
with whom they had difficulty dealing. The message from teachers, he said,
was "loud and clear," to deal with students as individuals, to deal with
the particular behavior:

> discussion mostly centered around the behavior; if the kid was a
> behavior problem, that's what you dealt with. If, you know, if they
> were not a behavior problem, then it wasn't an issue, it didn't matter if
> they were sitting in the class purple [i.e., it didn't matter what color
> they were]. If they were purple, and they were acting out, then it was
> something to deal with because they were acting out. It wasn't an
> issue that you have to watch out for these students because they are
> black or because these students are white.

Dante seemed predisposed to accept this message and comfortably adopt
it as his own. In contrast to Dante, if Kirk consciously picked up on this
message, he didn't say, but the individualism it advocated seemed to serve
him as a lifesaver of sorts, as illustrated below.

Although Dante uses the language of curriculum differentiation rather
than individualization as do many contemporary educators, he is talking
about individualizing or adapting his teaching for particular students. The
individualizing is intended to help students meet common behavioral expectations and the New York State learning standards that Charter School
has adopted wholeheartedly and then score well on the New York State
English–language arts and mathematics standardized tests that begin in
4th grade. (Later, New York State testing for No Child Left Behind would
begin in 3rd grade.) It is also possible that the now widely used language
of differentiation is intended both to suggest something new or beyond
individualization and to resonate with the language of difference and diversity. In other words, differentiation suggests that one is doing something positive about differences among students.

I call the individualism observed at Charter School "radical" because it ignores, if not denies, group differences or identifications as if they do not matter—to the individual, to the group, or to learning. A less radical individualism would acknowledge and be responsive to group differences and identifications that are important to the individual and/or the group while emphasizing individual behavior, accomplishments, and problems. Moreover, radical individualism in this instance appears to further conformity (not unlike the early Jesuits) and basic skills much more than creativity, critical thinking, and cultural expression.

Kirk: "Shell Shock"

Kirk was a member of the same cohort of prospective teachers at Charter School as Dante. He worked with a 5th-grade class on the second floor and gave no indication of sharing Dante's concerns about being a male elementary teacher. His major concerns, he told us, were about reaching out to students who "don't really respond well to any teacher" and dealing with "city kids and stuff like that." Kirk described the students who seem not to respond well as "kids that are almost like the outcasts," who also lack parental support and/or learning capacity. The "city kids" were poor kids lacking adequate clothing and cleanliness. Kirk also was concerned about working with these students' parents, since he neither wanted to anger them nor "to look bad" himself. Initially, groups and group differences were quite salient and intimidating for Kirk.

His elementary school experience was "like 99% white students," Kirk said, and the majority of students where his mother teaches (and where he has done some volunteer work) are white, so walking into Charter School was completely different, "like complete shell shock." He referred to "the ethnic diversity and stuff like that" as new to him and Charter School as a school where "the whites are almost, like, outnumbered." The "stuff like that," which Kirk mentioned more than once, appears to refer to relative poverty and a perceived lack of parental support and caring, both of which Kirk later claimed are more influential than race with respect to how much students can learn. He compared two students to illustrate this claim:

> we have one student [apparently black] who's very bright, who's a very bright kid, but he was a behavior problem all the time, but he had a really bad family life, like really bad stuff going on at home. But he was really smart, but he didn't get good grades in school. While we had a white student who was, I mean, very, mom was involved and everything like that. And he was a very, probably about equally as

smart, but he performed awesome in school because he wasn't disruptive. I mean, he was always on task and I just, maybe the income level or maybe the parents working, having to work two jobs to be able to support people that is taking away from the kid and the family life at home, which was making them seem like they are dumber, you know, not really dumber but it makes it seem that way because they're not, their grades aren't reflecting their intelligence.

"So it didn't matter," Kirk concluded, "what color they were, it didn't matter at all." His emphasis on parental support and caring (e.g., seeing that homework was completed, that the child was clean and neat) may be a carryover from his own experience growing up with a single parent, or hearing his mother (who is a teacher) say similar things, or it may be a way of avoiding racialized distinctions and being seen as racist.

Positive experiences at Charter School and his own willingness to learn and change undermined but did not overturn Kirk's initial fears of people different from himself as well as his negative stereotypes. He described the change this way:

I just never had the chance to work with, like, a different minority of students, and it's actually kind of cool because I, I don't know, I've learned a lot from just the kids . . . the way they talk and the way they learn is, like, completely different from the way I learned . . . just give every single kid a chance, like, a fair shot.

Asked what he had learned about dealing constructively with difference and diversity, Kirk said, "I don't think there's a, really should be a way to deal with it." Instead, he described himself as "teaching each child . . . everyone is different . . . everyone is equal and no, like, no matter the skin color [or] background, everyone's the same." In terms of teaching the class, Kirk said:

I should just treat it as just a normal classroom. I shouldn't be, she [his co-op] shouldn't have to deal with it as "Well let's look at this 'cause I have, like, seven black boys and six black girls," and, like, I shouldn't have to deal with it that way. It should just be dealt as, as "this is my class."

From fear and negative stereotypes, particularly of African American students, Kirk moved to a radical individualist and colorblind perspective. If one ignores or denies the importance of racialized or ethnic (or other group) membership to focus on the individual, and treats everyone equally (i.e., the same), one dilutes fears or biases rather than facing them directly. Colorblindness also tends to assume that middle-class white norms are appropriate standards for everyone, although their whiteness may be invisible to the person who claims not to "see color." This is evident in Kirk's repeated use of the words *should* and *shouldn't* and his reference to a "normal classroom" in the excerpt just quoted.

Asked how his ideas and beliefs about student difference and diversity changed over the semester of Field Experience, Kirk responded, "I would say I'm a lot more open to a lot more, a lot of difference, seeing the different students." An example he offered was sitting in on a parent-teacher conference about a Chinese student, with a translator present. "You just have to figure out a way to be able to connect with everybody . . . just give 'em a chance." He reiterated that when he walked into Charter School, he did not have much background or knowledge about people who are different from himself. Now, he says, he does not "think there's really a, a difference [between what black and white children can learn]. . . . I think if you have it at home [parental support], and you have the right teaching, the diversity isn't really gonna matter too much."

When Kirk added that even students who lack "the basic, like, essentials, like not being, like, showered and not being clean and with the same clothes, like . . . they can still learn," it was unclear whether he was referring to black students or to all students. Asked how he would teach the students who "don't have the greatest home life," Kirk said he would "teach them the same way" and "teach them how to take responsibility for their own actions," such as homework and bathing, since there would not be someone at home to encourage or supervise them.

It was only later, after he had completed his Field Experience and first student-teaching placement at Charter School and was at a suburban school for his second placement, that Kirk acknowledged the depth of his fear and stereotypes about African American students. In response to the direct question "So what were your initial fears?", after several false starts, Kirk said:

> I thought that they [African American students] weren't going to like me, and I wasn't going to accept them as well. . . . "You're the, you're the white guy, I'm the black kid," and, and I wasn't gonna like it at all. That's all I was kinda worried about, I guess.

But, he said, "just take time to get, get to know 'em" and it is "just like talking to anybody, you know . . . you just don't look at skin color anymore." Opportunities for informal interaction with students helped Kirk get to know them and feel more at ease, but he still seemed awkward when he talked about African American students.

Give every kid a chance 'cause you'll be surprised which ones, which kids you think you'll get along most with. You know, me, like, kid growing up in the suburbs with all white friends, you would think I would get along with the white boys the most and it was actually African American girls that I got along with the most. I mean, it just [a 5-second pause, approximately], I guess, I don't know, looking back, I guess I grew up around a, in like, not out of prejudice, but it was just, that was the way it was, you know? We didn't have that to, like, we didn't have them, those like, I didn't have African, African American people in my school so I didn't have to really worry about but then, giving them the chance, I, you realize that yeah, they're just, you know, every normal, normal persons, you know, nothing different.

If African Americans are "normal persons . . . nothing different," then one does not need to confront color or African American-ness. Blacks become individuals, "like us" normal white people.

It would be difficult to find a clearer illustration of normalizing whiteness, that is, of setting middle-class white behavior as the norm or standard against which others are judged and/or to which they should aspire. In such cases, claims to not see color tend to mean seeing and treating people as white or assuming that they will or "should" act like (usually idealized notions of) white people. An important difference between Dante's and Kirk's versions of Radical Individualism is that Dante talked about differentiating the curriculum for individual students while Kirk talked about treating individual students the same way.

Despite his awkwardness in discussing race or color and his claims about student sameness, Kirk compared his 5th-grade Charter School students favorably to his second placement, 3rd-grade suburban students:

[A]t first I guess you stereotypically say that they're African American, they're minorities, they're poor and whatever, but after being there, and I'm going to this school now which is suburbial [sic] and a lot more wealthier, I feel like the other kids, just 'cause they didn't have money, I think they were just as easy to teach if, and more fun and you know, I, those, they had way more personality than these kids at this new school have, and I almost find these kids at this school boring. I mean, the other kids have so much, so diverse backgrounds, so they have so many different stories that they bring. . . . [T]hey had more personality than the kids I have now.

Charter School fostered constructive social interaction as well as book-learning, and Charter School students were "a lot more open with you . . .

a lot easier to talk to. . . . we found more things in common," such as music, sports, movies, and growing up with one parent. It is significant, I believe, that Kirk used "we" in referring to "things in common." And he said that he thought that in the future he "would be okay with the classroom with different backgrounds. I don't really find it that much different."

In a relatively short period of time, Kirk made substantial changes in his outlook and interaction with black students—from distance, negative stereotypes, and fear to declaring them not "that much different," apparently from white students. He described his racially/ethnically/culturally diverse Charter School 5th graders in nonracial terms such as "just as easy to teach," "more fun," and having "way more personality" than the mostly white suburban 3rd graders at his second student-teaching placement. In an important sense, Kirk moved from "over-emphasizing" race (for example, exaggerating the proportion of African American students at Charter School) to, in effect, not seeing race very much, if at all. Kirk eased his fears and stereotypes in large part by erasing race, by avoiding or denying it and focusing on treating individual students equally rather than on facing his fears and biases. He also seems to have redefined differences among groups of students at Charter School in terms of cleanliness or parental support, which may be rough proxies for racial or social class differences, although they do not mirror racial or class divisions.

Kirk's resolution appeared to be an enthusiastic adoption of the prevailing individualist ethos at Charter School that Dante described as "it didn't matter if they [students] were sitting in the class purple." One wonders what might have happened if the school's prevailing ethos were more responsive to color and culture in teacher-student and intergroup relations instead of "whiting it out," that is, whether Kirk might have made further changes toward accepting diversity and building on it. (Our observations indicate that the curriculum at Charter School was inclusive of color and culture in a matter-of-fact way, for example, in the stories included in reading–language arts materials.)

SYLVIA AND ETHAN

Sylvia and Ethan also tended toward Radical Individualism, but in a less clear-cut and consistent manner than Dante and Kirk. Overall, the specifics they provided belied their general statements and claims. Sylvia seemed to be trying to present herself as open to difference and diversity, which she said are "just completely normal." Although Charter School is much more diverse than her elementary school, "it's the norm nowadays," which she dealt with by individualizing but still recognizing group membership.

Ethan, a prospective English teacher at Royalton High School, was the most self-referential of all the prospective teachers in the cohorts we followed and a self-proclaimed individualist. He wanted to be seen and treated as an individual and, in turn, he said, to treat his students as individuals.

Neither prospective teacher mentioned student difference or diversity as a concern in anticipating student-teaching at Charter School or Royalton. Sylvia described her major concern as teaching the intense, rigorous reading program with 1st graders, "making sure I hit all the kids' needs." More generally, she expressed concern about meeting her cooperating teacher's expectations. Ethan shared three concerns: talking to students as adults while maintaining his authority; "being human," by which he meant burping or bumping into something and then "gain[ing] your respect back"; and being "too idealistic." Rarely did Ethan talk about his own teaching or interactions with students, other than informal or social ones, which he described positively. Instead, he would redirect conversation to himself and, for example, his very strict father and his own high school years.

Illustrative of Sylvia's awkwardness with difference and the apparent contradictions between her general and specific statements is the following comment about a daily reading activity in her cooperating teacher's 1st-grade classroom where two students are selected "to do, like, a special reading" of their choice:

> And, um, one of the girls yesterday brought in a book that had African American children in it. So, it's never an issue, and it's never a concern here. Diversity is just completely normal. . . . I don't really know any other way to describe it, you know, like you see, um, the Caucasian and African American girls walking down the, the hallway holding hands or, um, you know, you see maybe, um the Russian boy helping, um, you know, the Spanish girl pick up her crayons on the floor. It's just, there's never an issue, it's never a concern, you know. If someone doesn't succeed at something, they never use their race or their diversity as an excuse why they just can't handle it.

Later, Sylvia added, "So the kids just, um, accept everyone for who they are. It's [where you're from or what you look like] never a discussion here, and that's the one thing I like about it."

Difference and diversity may be less of an issue for Charter School students than for Sylvia whose language sounds stilted (e.g., *Caucasian, Spanish*) and whose assumptions about using race as an excuse seem directed toward "them," not "us." Personally, I wince at the use of the word *Caucasian*, which, like *Caucasoid, Mongoloid*, and *Negroid*, are part of the old, discredited racial language. My predominantly white university students tell me, when I ask about their use of the language and indicate its origins, that they thought it was not only acceptable but more polite than "white" and less cumbersome than "European American." I suspect that it is also a way, perhaps unrecognized by my students until we talk about it, of avoiding whiteness and its accompanying privilege.

Sylvia seemed conflicted about "certain, particular cultural groups hav[ing] different expectations," for example, about personal space and the importance of family dinners together that might interfere with doing homework. How do you respect cultural traditions and school expectations? Sylvia's response was "to be sensitive to the needs, individual needs of everybody." She also said that she found these questions both difficult to talk about and to handle in the classroom: "Like, man, it's such a hard topic to talk about." Yet, just a few minutes later, Sylvia recounted:

> I didn't really start interacting with any diversity until I started working at my job, um, on the ambulance and until I was able to, um, work with the city clientele and interact with schools such as this. . . . I was accepting to everything, but maybe it's so normal to me that I don't even notice it anymore.

Toward the end of her student-teaching at Charter School, Sylvia described her openness to diversity in terms of not expressing bias:

> I was very open to diversity last fall, and I can, I think, I am so much more open to it now. Out of all the diversity that was in my class, there was never a time where I looked at someone and said, and gave a stereotypical comment of why they weren't able to succeed at the lesson, or why they weren't able to do it.

Although Sylvia said that she did not really see or hear any messages about diversity at Charter School, the teachers were "pretty respectful" around her and "everything I have noticed so far has been equal, you know, across the board" with some ability-based differentiation. She gave an example of her co-op providing extra help and encouragement to a student who "couldn't write for anything when she first started."

By the end of the academic year, Sylvia seemed to have adopted the Radical Individualism toward which she appeared to have been heading. She told us that "when we talk about diverse students, I automatically think of culture, and I don't think that is going to be a problem at all because I treat all kids equally. . . . I found a lot of options to meet the diverse needs, even those that are struggling academically." She concluded that her experience working in the city in an after-school program and on an ambulance "really helped me to relate to those children such as the poverty level and the low incomes and the dirty clothes and what not. Many of those things aren't their [the students'] fault, they have no control over them." Like Kirk, Sylvia has erased race.

What makes Ethan's adoption of Radical Individualism noteworthy is that he wants it for himself and seems to ascribe that desire to other students without any evidence or reasoning except to say that, for example, a unit on black authors or attention to black issues disrespects the white minority. He told me that:

> people want to be treated as themselves, people want their own identity. . . . I am sick of talking about diversity, granted I am a black kid who grew up in [suburban New York City], I have had my fill of diversity. I am diversity. . . . [L]et's talk about individual diversity. Let's talk about what makes each and everybody unique. . . . Because once everybody's an individual, once everybody is treated with individual respect, then you don't have to talk about diversity because now people are people, which is the way it was meant to be in the first place.

Ethan's seemingly urgent plea reminded me of some of the high school juniors and seniors I interviewed in the late 1990s about their social identities. I asked them how they would describe themselves, and then about the meaning of the descriptors they mentioned. Approximately 30% of the students rejected racialized group labels; a subset of these students rejected all group labels. Their reasons were primarily that the categorizations were divisive; the students seemed to think that eliminating the categories and being "individuals" would also eliminate stereotypes, intergroup tensions, and divisiveness.

Blake, a student from a school in the same urban district where Ethan was doing his student-teaching, described himself as "a person first," and spoke angrily about racial slurs and the negative media portrayal of blacks, especially black males like himself. While neither denying nor ignoring being black, Blake emphasized that he should be treated fairly as another human being and equally as an American. He wanted to be seen as a person with rights and feelings like anyone else, instead of being stereotyped as a black male likely to cause trouble.

In response to our question about what it means to him to be an American, Blake emphasized that he "should be equal to any other person in this country . . . be given the same opportunities, whether it be employment, schooling, or whatever." Echoing Martin Luther King Jr., Blake continued:

And I should not be singled out or just treated differently or treated any less than any other person. It should be based on my character, and the content of it. And that's what I feel it should be to be an American, but today, in today's times, it seems that to be an American to me is almost a joke. (quoted in Cornbleth, 2003, p. 40)

The students who rejected racialized or ethnic group labels saw the categorizations as the source of problems for both individuals and groups and appeared to favor what I called a "resort to individualism" to avoid and/or oppose racism and other forms of division and discrimination (Cornbleth, 2003, p. 53). A resort to individualism is, however, double-edged. For example, endorsing traditional U.S. individualism—rugged, possessive, or otherwise—deflects attention from institutional or structural aspects of racism and intergroup conflict. The high school students and prospective teachers like Ethan may be undermining their own possibilities in the longer run by seeming to take a conservative individualist position that effectively sustains racial/ethnic hierarchy and hostility while it seems to offer more equal opportunities to individuals.

Although acknowledging, for example, that it is important to some black students whether or not another teacher or adult at Royalton is black, Ethan said that after Field Experience, he was "more firm" about not wanting to deal with any form of difference and diversity except individual. "I always considered myself an individualist. I considered myself one who wants to deal with people on a person-to-person basis, and that's how I relate to the world." "I'm not saying that you shouldn't understand culture," he continued, "understanding culture will go a long way in understanding individuals, you know . . . but, I think we tend to get carried away." The example he gave, however, seemed to illustrate both cultural and individual insensitivity. One of the assigned readings in a teacher education class, he told us, was about teaching Chinese students:

because apparently Chinese kids have a tendency to be quiet, and teachers take that as a sign of disrespect when the students are shy, not as disrespect, but as, they take it as a sign that they're not reaching the students when really, you know, the Chinese culture, the students are just being respectful. Understood. But it seems to me, like, you could just circumvent all that if the teachers just walked up to the students and said, "hey, what's going on?" you know, then, then the teacher, after getting to know the student would realize that the students are understanding the materials and would therefore not have doubts about whether or not he is being effective, he or she is being effective to the student.

Ethan's example and his use of group labels (e.g., black, white, Chinese) suggest that his individualism may be largely for himself. Not only was he more self-referential than the other prospective teachers, but Ethan also was among the least reflective about his own practice and its effects. He did not seem to learn, grow, and/or change substantially during the academic year, except perhaps to become less idealistic about what he could accomplish as a teacher and to realize that he needed to be firmer with students. In his words, "I walked in extremely idealistic; good, I'm glad I got that knocked out of me."

THE DOWNSIDES OF RADICAL INDIVIDUALISM

Before turning to the downsides of Radical Individualism, a review of its advantages for prospective and new teachers will suggest why its disadvantages tend to be overlooked. The advantages explicitly stated or clearly inferred in conversations with prospective teachers are of three broad types: curricular, teaching, and personal. Cross-cutting these are the assumed advantage of not being or being seen as racist and the advantage of Radical Individualism's compatibility with what seemed to be the prevailing ethos at Charter School.

Curricular advantages include meeting diverse students' needs in ability, preferred learning modality, and/or kind of intelligence by "differentiating your curriculum" or individualizing instruction (Dante, Sylvia). "Cultural" differences (usually referring to racial/ethnic, SES, and language) can be acknowledged, linked with learning differences, and subsumed by curriculum differentiation (Dante, Sylvia). Another and perhaps opposite kind of curricular advantage follows from Kirk's position that race does not matter and should not have to be considered. Giving each student the same opportunity to learn not only is fair in this view but also relatively easy, since curriculum differentiation on any basis requires time and effort.

Two teaching advantages were mentioned. One is that you will be a more successful teacher if you differentiate the curriculum to provide access and support for all students (Dante). A second is that if racial and other group-linked differences do not matter, you can teach just about anyone, anywhere (Kirk, Sylvia).

Personal advantages of Radical Individualism, not surprisingly, varied with the individual prospective teacher. In the cases of Kirk and Ethan, their own ascribed race did seem to matter, insofar as it can be seen as leading them to Radical Individualism, Kirk because he might be seen as the bad white guy and Ethan because he did not want to be seen as African American. Dante, in contrast, was outgoing and sociable, describing himself as someone who easily establishes positive interpersonal relationships with other people. Approaching students as individuals, then, and adopting a Radical Individualism were familiar and comfortable for him. Sylvia, in contrast, was still awkward talking about difference and diversity, but wanted to present herself as open to it. Radical Individualism provided that entry. Kirk, who had little experience with people different from himself, was initially fearful and stereotypically negative about Charter School's diverse student population. For him, Radical Individualism was like a life jacket. It enabled him to ignore racialized groups and focus on individuals and less personally threatening descriptors such as differences in parental support or personal cleanliness.

For Ethan, all the advantages of Radical Individualism were personal. It allowed him to distance himself from African Americans and, at least in his own mind, from racial stereotypes and discriminatory treatment as well. He would have his own identity, and talking about diversity would be unnecessary.

There are at least two major downsides to Radical Individualism as a response to student difference and diversity. One is that it too often fosters conformity. Despite the rhetoric of individualization, differentiation, or curriculum adaptation, Radical Individualism is an assimilationist path. A second, related downside is that Radical Individualism both reflects and fosters a colorblindness that tends to assume and sustain white, middle-class norms, standards, and privilege. Standards (and accompanying assessments) become standardizing (see, e.g., Sleeter, 2005). Although I emphasize race here, similar or parallel arguments could be made for class, gender, language, religion, and sexual orientation.

Individualism as Conformist

Individualism has a long and celebrated, even mythic, history in the United States. Its educational equivalent, individualization, was a dominant slogan or theme in 20th-century elementary education, along with educating the "whole child." Meeting individual student needs became an unquestioned piety among educators. That the individual student rarely was consulted about her or his "needs" or how best to meet them went largely unnoticed, except perhaps by students. In practice, individualization has been relatively thin (e.g., allowing students to work their way through a language arts or math workbook or program at their own pace) and, in fact, usually has been directed toward conformity with common behavioral and "learning" goals or standards more than toward developing individual interests or talents. It is in this sense that Radical Individualism is assimilationist. All students are to take up the expected behavior and knowledge.

Learning "appropriate school behavior" and "school knowledge" that meets state–defined academic standards can be useful accomplishments, of course, even if they have little to do with fostering individual uniqueness as the language suggests.

My sense is that the prospective teachers at Charter School were naïve, largely ignorant of the implications of the Radical Individualism, which they picked up on and appeared to adopt. It sounded fair, offered help to students who were judged to need extra assistance, and did not reveal or challenge any teacher biases. By not facing student differences and diversity other than differences in behavior and cognitive ability, radical individualism can serve to discourage individualization. Individualization discourse also can mask deficit assumptions about individual students and groups of students who are not "like us," and, in so doing, serve as a cover for various forms of bias.

Individualism as Colorblind

Racial colorblindness has been variously defined, for example, as literally not seeing a person's color, as ignoring color or believing it doesn't matter, and as not talking about color (what Pollock [2004] calls "colormute"), as if talk about color or racial groups was taboo or an indicator of one's own racism. I am reminded of the fable of the three monkeys who cover their eyes, ears, or mouth in order to "see no evil, hear no evil, speak no evil." The phrase or proverb "see no evil, hear no evil, speak no evil" has been used to describe someone who wants to avoid a difficult situation or "look the other way." While the saying could be interpreted as not participating in evil, "do no evil," it also can be interpreted as indicating that not recognizing and interrupting evil serves to sustain it.

In historically color-conscious U.S. society, literally not seeing and responding to a person's color or physical appearance is difficult, if not impossible, unless one is severely visually impaired. The colorblindness of Radical Individualism is primarily of the second variety: trying to ignore color and believe it makes no difference. This form of colorblindness is widespread in the United States, especially among white elementary teachers who claim to see only individual children (e.g., Marx, 2006; Schofield, 2001; Sleeter, 1993). For example, one of the teachers in Sleeter's 2-year staff development project told an interviewer:

> What's the big hangup, I really don't see this color until we start talking about it, you know. I see children as having differences, maybe they can't write their numbers or they can't do this or they can't do that, I don't see the color until

we start talking multicultural. Then, oh yes, that's right, he's this and she's that. (quoted in Sleeter, 1993, p. 161)

Another simply said, "I really believe elementary teachers feel that kids are kids" (1993, p. 161). Sleeter makes an especially astute observation about the claims of not seeing color when she says that:

> *People do not deny seeing what they actually do not see.* Rather, they profess to be color-blind when trying to suppress negative images they attach to people of color, given the significance of color in the U.S., the dominant ideology of equal opportunity, and the relationship between race and observable measures of success. (Sleeter, 1993, pp. 161–162 emphasis added).

When prospective or newer teachers (or veterans) say that they do not see color, that race does not matter, or that they treat all students the same, one might ask whom they treat their students the same as—the same as whom? Most often, middle-class white culture and students are assumed to be the norm, which serves to further advantage or privilege white people. This assumption often goes unnoticed so that whiteness remains invisible, which is a major source of its power to dominate everyday "common sense." Deciding that skin color does not or should not matter allows whites to ignore the advantages of whiteness as well as the experiences of people of color. Colorblindness is not race-neutral.

What has been called "colortalk" about race and difference (e.g., Thompson, 1999) was quite limited among prospective teachers who followed a Radical Individualist path. Although I sensed that the prospective teachers at Charter School realized that they were trying to avoid facing racialized differences among students and groups of students, I doubt that they thought about possible negative consequences, such as sustaining racial hierarchy and white privilege.

Schofield (1982, 2001) has clearly illustrated important consequences of what she calls a colorblind perspective, based on her 4-year field study of an urban middle school constructed to be a model of racially integrated public education. She noted that few teachers or other school personnel anticipated or recognized the consequences of their colorblind perspective, either positive or negative. Consequences that were more positive for adults included: (1) reducing the potential for overt conflict over disparities in treatment or outcomes that could be seen as race-related (and, thus, protecting the school from discrimination charges); (2) minimizing awkwardness, anxiety, or embarrassment of faculty (and students) who had little prior experience in desegregated schools or communities, thus helping to sustain a "veneer of politeness" (2001, p. 258) and personal comfort; and

(3) increasing teachers' freedom of action and simplifying decision making by not having to explicitly consider race and, in so doing, possibly fostering an environment that is conducive to racially discriminatory behavior (because explanations for racial inequalities other than race are less likely to be questioned). Negative consequences, primarily for students, included: (1) ignoring the impact of cultural differences among students on how they act in school; and (2) failing to respond to and build on diversity.

The last two—the negative consequences of colorblindness—are particularly relevant to teacher education and the experiences of prospective and newer teachers facing difference and diversity. With respect to ignoring the likely impact of cultural differences among students, Schofield (2001) cites research, including her own, that shows black and white cultural differences associated with (1) black male students seeing "ambiguously aggressive acts as less mean and threatening and as more playful and friendly" than did white students (2001, p. 260); (2) differing classroom discussion styles that might mistakenly interpret black student involvement as belligerence; and (3) greater familiarity with the kinds of questions that elementary teachers typically ask among middle-class white students. Schofield concludes that teachers who appropriate a colorblind perspective "may rule out awareness and use of information that would be helpful in deciding how best to structure materials in ways that work well for the range of students they teach as well as in interpreting many aspects of their students' behavior" (2001, p. 261). When that colorblind perspective is effectively white, white privilege is sustained.

Now, student diversity extends beyond black and white to encompass a range of racial/ethnic groups as well as other differences. Colorblindness (or presumed gender-blindness or class-blindness) deprives teachers of even more cultural knowledge to support teaching and learning and on which to build culturally relevant curriculum, for example, by securing and using materials that reflect and appeal to varied student interests, life experiences, and heritages. As a result, all students suffer an unnecessarily narrow education. Similar, negative effects of racial colorblindness have been noted in related areas such as counseling (e.g., Neville, Spanierman, & Doan, 2006) and by organizations such as the American Psychological Association (APA, 2003).

Ignoring race both within and outside schools does not remove racism's prior and continuing effects. Colorblindness enables teachers and others to ignore or perhaps not even recognize institutionalized racism (or sexism and other forms of discriminatory treatment), apart from individual bigotry. Institutionalized forms of racism are built into the educational or other system and, over time, come to be taken for granted as natural or normal, and consequently, become largely invisible. Examples of institutionalized racism are Eurocentric textbooks and other materials, tracking systems that enable white students to dominate the highest track (or reading group), and forms of classroom discourse and interaction that are more familiar to middle-class white students than to other groups. Rather than interrupting racist practices (see, e.g., Tatum, 1997), colorblind perspectives tend to rationalize and maintain racial hierarchy and white privilege. More on confronting colorblindness is offered in Chapter 7.

CONCLUSIONS

Given Kirk's initial fears and negative stereotypes, Sylvia's awkwardness and seemingly unacknowledged stereotypes, and Dante's concern with being accepted as a male elementary teacher, it appears unlikely that any of them would have resisted the pull of Radical Individualism at Charter School, at least initially, even if they had been urged and helped to do so. Moreover, gaining acceptance and support from faculty and other school personnel in exchange for fitting in was too attractive a bargain, even if it was unrecognized as such.

Although Radical Individualism does not face student difference and diversity very constructively, especially in the longer run, it may be acceptable as a temporary position on a continuing path toward more constructive engagement. The conformist and colorblind aspects of Radical Individualism seem to ease initial adjustment while impeding the longer-term development of positive relationships with students and the lessening of inequities. New teachers' understandings, experiences, and responses or approaches to difference and diversity are in flux and are amenable to change, as the cases here have illustrated. Once past their initial fears and stereotypes, prospective and newer teachers (and other professionals) are likely to be more open to alternatives; they can be supported for the changes they have made thus far and encouraged to continue on.

For example, new teachers can learn to examine their own and others' assumptions and the implications of alternative courses of action toward the goal of facing difference and dealing with it more constructively for all concerned. Questions for consideration might include: When we don't "see" race or don't think it matters, what assumptions are we making? How might race and racism affect teaching? Learning? How might treating "all students the same" be unfair, advantaging some students and disadvantaging others? What forms of individualism am I using? In what ways do they engage students' interests and promote their talents? How do they foster conformity and assimilation to middle-class white (or other) norms and standards?

Such conversations require major changes in teacher education beliefs and practices in some settings. While drafting this chapter of *Diversity and the New Teacher*, I received a flyer from the school of education at a private college in the area offering a teaching fellowship of $30,000 per year to a doctoral student with at least 3 years of K–12 teaching experience and "the expertise and experience to raise our [teacher] candidates' awareness of different teaching and learning styles shaped by cultural influences and assist them in developing teaching strategies which will be effective for all students." The fellowship, again according to the flyer, is associated with the college's "diversity initiative," and "embraces the value of incorporating diverse perspectives." This is the most explicit language in the flyer, and it seemed to communicate mixed messages. Are the lack of specific references to racialized or ethnic, SES, gender, language, religion, ability, and other differences to be considered unnecessary or understood? Impolite? Or, might the college just be looking for a person "of color" to "diversify" its largely white faculty?

In any event, teacher education programs that have been comfortably (for white teacher educators and prospective teachers) "colormute" might profitably engage in more "colortalk." Ignorance or silence does not equal innocence. Not naming, examining, and interrupting racism, sexism, and other forms of individual and/or institutionalized discrimination allows inequalities to continue and perhaps to grow wider while normalizing white privilege as meritorious. Thompson (1999) argues persuasively that colortalk is a much-needed "act of resistance to white hegemony" (p. 142). I concur, in the interests of our students, our students' students, and our society.

5

Worlds Apart

The "Worlds Apart" response to student difference and diversity is largely one of distance. After some efforts to make contact with students and establish productive working relationships, primarily on terms that are familiar to the prospective teachers, Ken and Lynn pretty much seemed to give up and opt for their own survival until the end of the student-teaching placement at Royalton High School. They saw the chasm between themselves and their students as too great or too difficult to be bridged. Schools like Royalton and its students, from this perspective, are "not like us" or "not like me," where us/me refers to a white, middle-class, academically prepared, and cooperative, if not well-motivated, student standard. The student "others" at Royalton and elsewhere might be seen as interesting or "fun," but they require control, according to this view, before you can teach them anything. And then, it is best to use structured, teacher-dominated instructional methods not only to maintain control but also because of students' weak knowledge and skill base.

Ken and Lynn were among the least successful prospective teachers in the cohorts we followed, along with Ethan, who was a self-proclaimed individualist as described in the previous chapter. Both of the PTs who are the focus of this chapter worked with the same cooperating teacher in science, Ken in year 1 of the project and Lynn in year 2. Although it may be tempting to attribute the PTs' experience at Royalton to their co-op, this is too simple an explanation. One reason given for placing these PTs with Nolan as their co-op was his reputation as a strong disciplinarian who got along with his students and was willing to work with PTs who seemed hesitant or lacking in self-confidence, as did Ken and Lynn. Another is that in the PTs' second, middle school placements, Lynn appeared to be much more successful than Ken, perhaps in part because she was placed in an affluent, predominantly white suburb while Ken remained in the city. The interaction of individual and institutional setting does not lend itself to linear or unidimensional accounts.

While Ken and Lynn represent only one-eighth of the prospective teachers we followed, their response to student difference and diversity is important because "Worlds Apart" seems quite similar to the perspective of the "negative teachers" at Royalton and other teachers at Royalton and elsewhere who are described as "burnt out." And Ken and Lynn are just beginning. Their response is also important because it is based on more than racialized differences. Social class figures prominently in these cases, as does student ability, apparent effort and motivation, and, of course, student behavior and cooperation or disruption. Moreover, the trajectory or path of their response to student difference and diversity can serve as a warning to other prospective and newer teachers so that they might recognize and avoid similar pitfalls.

Both Ken and Lynn attended high schools in predominantly white, affluent suburban communities—at opposite ends of the state. Ken described his school district as middle- to "more upper, upper-middle-class" and "majorly [sic] white," while Lynn described hers as "pretty well-to-do" and "mostly white." Both took advanced and AP (Advanced Placement) classes and had relatively little contact with students who did not. Lynn described her high school, in contrast to Royalton, as:

> a lot of academically minded people, probably I say that because I was one of them, so I saw a lot of academically minded people. I know there were other people who, you know, were not into school as much or whatever, um, and just as there are at [Royalton]. [Royalton] has the academically minded people too, but at [her high school] everybody was very, you know, if you're academically minded, you're very serious, um, you know, you're taking all of these AP courses, or some AP courses anyway. I don't even think that they offer AP courses [at Royalton].

Ken put it this way:

> I was always in the advanced classes, so I think the people who were the type that acted up weren't really involved in the classes I was in. The people in the advanced classes were kinda concentrated on learning, and that kind of stuff, but I guess there were always still the, the few troublemakers in the, in some of the classes.

Neither sounded boastful in describing their high school classes and fellow students. That was just their experience and what was familiar to them.

While Ken's high school was more traditional, Lynn's was built as open plan and minimally structured (e.g., no hall passes, no assigned seats at lunch). Both had more teaching-learning and extracurricular resources than Royalton.

In addition to high school experiences that were very different from what they found at Royalton, neither Ken nor Lynn had much prior experience working with children or young people. Even their limited experiences were primarily with middle-class whites like themselves. Their lives up to this point seemed sheltered or protected, if not isolated. Consequently, Royalton's location, student population, and limited resources were largely unfamiliar and anxiety-inducing. Lynn told us that when she was in high school:

> you weren't aware of poverty even though, you know, there may have been single parents or things like that I wasn't really aware of . . . and here we are learning, you know, these kids or a lot of them are on welfare or they might be the parent or the adult of the house.

Early in their Field Experience, both Ken and Lynn seemed to be moving past their pre-encounter and initial apprehensions about city schools and students, with good intentions for connecting with their students and teaching them science (see Chapter 2). Not long after they began student-teaching during second semester, however, they appeared to shift their focus to classroom management, which Ken called control or discipline, lowering their sights to getting by and just about giving up on teaching their students much science.

KEN: "VERY DIFFERENT FROM ME"

Ken told us that he expected urban students to be "a little more difficult" than suburban students, "but it adds a little more, um, excitement than kids sittin' around and listening, just, you know . . . not to say that [Royalton] kids have, have more personality, but they're just more expressive maybe and . . . more stuff happens." Ken went on to say that he enjoyed his Field Experience at Royalton High School even though he never pictured himself in an urban school, and that he liked the students personally. They were not as "troublesome," causing problems all the time, as he had anticipated. "I guess that's a common stereotype of urban schools, and it, it does occur, but it's not as much as I pictured in my head." Ken's recognition of "a common stereotype" was one of very few indications of reflection on his own behavior or empathy for others.

The behavior that Ken found troublesome or disruptive was in-class "acting up," for example, "the girls would talk to each other and laugh and stuff" while "the guys would, you know, be throwing stuff sometimes [e.g., paper wads, a pencil] and just kind of wandering around, not even paying attention at all." Ken also was disturbed by students who did not seem to pay attention or participate in class; he attributed such behavior to their not caring about school. Compared to other prospective teachers at Royalton, Ken did relatively little to try to encourage his students to "care" and participate constructively in his class. Compare, for example, his interpretation of student behavior and response with Amanda's (see Chapter 2).

During this early period, Ken said that he did not see much diversity among the students at Royalton "'cause almost the entire school is African American–Hispanic" with "some white students, very few Asians," so there "wasn't that much diversity between the students." Ken went on to say that he did not have experience dealing with "diversity between myself and having African American students," and that he did not think that you "can account for them being the way they are [as described above] because they're African American." Since most of the students were African American, so were the students Ken saw as troublemakers. He did not offer possible reasons for the student behavior that troubled him or, conversely, for why certain behaviors that other teachers might ignore or deal with routinely troubled him.

Ken cited three major challenges as he looked toward student-teaching, the greatest being "controlling the students and, I guess [the second], trying to get the students engaged in the, in the lesson." Later, he also mentioned subject-matter knowledge as a challenge. He found some of his students' questions puzzling and his cooperating teacher very knowledgeable. My sense was that the puzzling questions were on the order of "why is that?" or "how could that be?", which Ken had not previously encountered or considered.

With respect to control and engaging his students, Ken recognized that:

> you need to set rules and enforce them. . . . I think if you get the students to start out, sit down and, and do some work right away, do like a question or two on the board or something, it'll get them kinda settled down, and then . . . bring stuff into the, into the lesson that they'll find relative to them, to their own lives. Or, stuff like . . . experiments or stuff that, that'll, like, fascinate them, that'll make them more interested in learning about it.

Later, Ken added that "you just need to put in an effort to connect with the students and get to know them . . . and that also helps you bring the lesson, to get them interested in a lesson." He did this in part by asking students to complete a questionnaire about their interests:

just to try to get them to write down the kind of stuff they like so I can
figure out the, any themes and stuff, and it seems like a lot of them
have the same kind of interests that I had [as a high school student,
e.g., sports, movies, talking on the phone] . . . so it's still your typical
high school students.

Ken seemed to find some comfort in the similarities. He went on to say that
a teacher should be friendly, but not a friend, to the students and should
show interest in them. Otherwise, "if the students feel like they're, the
teacher doesn't care about them, and they're just standing in front of a class
giving them information, they're not gonna pay attention, they're not gonna
care that much."

After this generally promising, even if sometimes simplistic, conversation, Ken returned to "the control thing" and said that he also was "kinda
worried about the respect part of it," because he was not that much older
than his students. Asked about how he might generate respect, Ken responded that he would show that he was the boss (see Chapter 2). Ken
concluded:

I am uncomfortable now [just prior to student-teaching], but I think that
it's just that you need to adjust to it and once I'm, you know, a few weeks
in, or however long it takes, and I get used to the students and know
what I need to do, I think I'll get, it'll be more comfortable after that.

Unfortunately, Ken became less, not more, comfortable with his students and seemed not to follow most of the advice he offered earlier about
what he should or would do. While age-related respect was not the issue
he thought it might be, and students did not ask many questions (Ken said
that he referred those questions he could not answer to his co-op), controlling "certain students" during class was even more of a challenge, even
though he had come to know the students and they him.

It's, it's people talking during class, people not paying attention. A lot
[clears throat], a lot of the kids just don't care, so they won't take notes,
they won't even take their tests [quizzes at the beginning of class], they
just hand in their tests blank. Just, mostly just interrupting the class and
talking to each other. . . . [J]ust the talking, more than anything.

Ken's response to the talking and other student behaviors he found disruptive was to try to increase control by writing up and kicking out a
disruptive student, which "kinda quiets down the rest of the class too."
The quieting effects, however, appeared to be only temporary. Ken did not

seem to connect student misbehavior with his instructional strategies. Although he did make use of one of the school's two video projectors to show some "short clips off the Internet," his lessons were primarily teacher talk and "giving notes." He told us:

> it's still basically just using the white board during class. I use the white board . . . basically when I'm giving a lesson. But I tell 'em they don't need to copy notes while I'm giving the lesson. And then I put up the notes afterwards on the overhead projector [for students to copy].

I have never understood the logic of this rather common instructional sequence. Students do not need to do any reading that may have been assigned, usually for homework, or pay attention during "the lesson" if the information they need to know for exams will be given to them (on the board, an overhead, or PowerPoint) at the end of the class period. It almost invites students to "act up" or doze off during "the lesson" and then "copy notes."

Bellwork became quizzes based on the previous day's classwork, and Ken only used two experiments involving water because, he said, the sink in his classroom was not working. Recall his lament about the time and effort required to go halfway down the hall to get a bucket of water, and compare his response to Amanda's outrage with the lack of books for her English students to take home to read/study (see Chapter 2). Making the content relevant was just "really hard," Ken said. An exception was the activity about respiration (described in Chapter 2) that Ken said the students liked.

Why Ken did not seem to make a stronger connection between such activities and student interest (paying attention, and so forth), and consider them worth the effort remains unclear. The closest he came was near the end of his student-teaching at Royalton, when Ken told us that control became less of a problem as he got to know his students. Then, seeming rather puzzled, he said, "they did like doing activities more than sitting there and taking notes and stuff, and working in groups usually kind of helped . . . they paid attention more, but they were still a little more talkative and everything." Ken then returned to the need "to be strict with them" and maintain control. Despite seemingly good intentions, he apparently believed that "discipline problems just keep me from teaching." Ken did not satisfactorily resolve the conflict he saw among student interest and engagement, control, and learning science. About academics, he concluded, "Kinda teach 'em the bare minimum that they need to know."

During Ken's student-teaching, when control was "even more of a challenge," Ken's language seemed to change, from referring to "students" to referring to "they" and "them." Talking about instructional activities, he continued to refer to "students" some of the time. Talking about control, however, he usually referred to "they" and "them," as if distancing himself from his students. In an uncomfortable sense, some students had become the opposition, if not the enemy.

Ken's conversation about his experience with difference and diversity at Royalton is consistent with the distancing interpretation, the distancing being vertical. Ken and his students were not simply different or far apart; they were beneath him. He was surprisingly open about his feelings, and awkward rather than arrogant expressing them. Ken's initial response to our question about working with student difference and diversity once he had begun student-teaching was that he did not find a difference. "No, I, I don't see it as any different than, you know, working with, you know, all people of my race or all different. I don't really see a difference between the two." Ken's response was not as disingenuous as it might seem, because it turns out that he distances the white students as well as the African American and Hispanic ones. When we asked about how his ideas or beliefs about difference and diversity had changed since the beginning of the school year, he responded at length:

> Um, I think that, if anything, the people of different diversity [*sic*] are how I pictured it. But the people of my race are actually more, are very different from me and more like the people of other races. . . . Like, I feel, like, white people are very different in this school than the white people that I know. They're more like the other people in the school, like, the other, like the other races in the school. They're, that's what they kinda act more like.

Asked for some examples, Ken said:

> Um, just more kind of [5-second pause], I don't wanna say, like, ghetto [laughs]. I don't know the right word to use. . . . [L]anguage and just the attitude . . . language is more, more, um, it's not grammatically correct, which I think is typical with whites that I associate with in my own normal life. And [8-second pause], um [5-second pause] . . . They're definitely on a different level than me. [Interviewer: OK, um, and the attitude?] It's kinda like more, more troublesome . . . like, thug-like [laughs], not all of them, but some of them.

When he came to Royalton, Ken expected such behavior from students of color, he said, and acknowledged negative stereotypes. He certainly did not expect such behavior from white students, assuming them to be like himself and his white friends.

At least two aspects of Ken's "confession" are noteworthy. One is that his critique of African American and Hispanic students is largely indirect, via the white students who act like "them," and confined to school behavior. Unlike other prospective teachers, he did not talk about home, street, or community conditions or cultures. Second, without mentioning social class or other types of difference that cross-cut racial/ethnic groupings, Ken is now recognizing differences among white students that he appears not to have encountered before. And the differences bother him.

He and his students are "Worlds Apart," and Ken seems to have little or no desire (or sense of how) to bridge those worlds. Yet he claimed that he was prepared to deal with difference and diversity because of his experiences with "a lot of minorities" who are "kinda stereotyped in the readings and stuff, and it's not necessarily like that." Ken usually qualified his negative characterizations as if to show that he was not prejudiced or "a racist." He appeared to be clueless regarding how his expressed beliefs and classroom behavior served to maintain racial and social-class hierarchy, including his own white, middle- to upper-middle-class privilege.

Later, asked how he felt his student-teaching at Royalton went overall, Ken was frank:

> I think that they put me with a very good teacher that I learned a lot about. I think that [3-second pause], I think it went kinda rough. . . . I look at it as a good learning experience, basically. . . . I don't see myself teaching in an urban school after this experience.

Ken saw himself working "in the same kind of high school" as he went to in the same, predominantly white, suburban area because "it's more educational and less discipline." He added

> the kids are on a different [PA announcement interrupts], the kids . . . care a lot more about the learning. . . . [T]ypically [the students] have plans to go on to college, and they wanna do as well as they can so that they can get in the better college, and I, I wanna be teaching more than controlling students.

The suburban students are more like Ken, from his world. Given Ken's inability and/or unwillingness to reach out to people who are different from himself, and to meet them at least halfway, it is just as well that he does not want to teach in an urban school. It is unlikely, however, that Ken can mask his biases so that he does not either pass them on to students in his classes and, in so doing, condone middle-class, suburban white students' biases, or diminish educational opportunities and outcomes for any students of color, students from working-class families, or students whose first language is not English.

With the help of some family connections, Ken obtained a teaching position in a selective, urban public high school on the East Coast. He was reported to be unhappy there and found a suburban teaching position for the following year.

LYNN: CULTURE AS CULPRIT

Although Lynn was apprehensive about dealing with Royalton High School students and their behavior, she said that she liked it there "in kind of a strange way," but she did not elaborate. Lynn was effusive about the school itself: "It's just a beautiful school . . . all the architecture and the history . . . all the beautiful, shining wood. It's just like 'wow'!"

Lynn was aware that "there are different cultures [at Royalton] so you can't relate to the people the same way," and referred to "this socioeco-nomic thing" and "different backgrounds, different experiences." Asked about change in her ideas or beliefs about difference and diversity since the beginning of the academic year, Lynn responded:

> I think that I have realized there is more a difference between people in terms of, like, their response to things or their cultures about different things than I had thought there was, but that we are all still people, and so they may act crazy or in ways that I don't understand, but there are reasons for why they are doing it. It is part of the culture. It is what they have grown up doing, um, it is part of their street behavior or something like that. And so it is not, you know, they are probably not trying to go against the system necessarily, you know, be crazy. I keep returning to the word *crazy*, it's just a kind of a, covers a lot of things. . . . It covers classroom chatter and, uh, loudness and getting up and walking around during class, little classroom misbehaviors . . . well, fighting wouldn't be quite crazy, it might be insanity [laughing] on a scale of craziness.

At the same time that she characterized fighting as insanity, Lynn com-mented that "I cannot expect them [her students] to be like me or what I have known or experienced in the past, so it is kind of wakening up that [in me]." She offered an example of two girls she had been watching in a class she was observing:

> This one girl was talking to her friend, and she just moved her head in a way that would have been, I would have taken as being kind of like,

uh, almost a hostile thing or an "in your face" type of thing, but her friend was, like, reacting like a friend would to someone that said [unintelligible] and not showing any of that feeling. So, it was like "wow"! That is probably just something that they might do in their family or in their culture or whatever that I have been misinterpreting.

Another example was about reasons why a student might have her/his head down during class:

They could be disinterested, they could be not caring about the school, but they also might not know how to read that well or not understand the material, so you gotta feeling of helplessness involved, so it's, you know, there could be bigger things at work. . . . You just need someone to dig around a little bit.

Despite these observations and insights, apprehension about student differences from her own experiences, along with being "on the quiet side" and "not a great first impression kind of person," seems to account for Lynn's reticence in getting to know and interacting with students during Field Experience. She told us:

I don't really know what to say to students one-on-one even though I have some ideas. . . . I think I am going to start talking to the ones that are just real close to me [while she is sitting in her CT's class and observing] 'cus I've been seeing them a lot on a regular basis, even just asking what their names are . . . taking it slow.

Lynn, like Ken, cited three major challenges at Royalton: "definitely the classroom management," connecting with students on a personal basis, and lesson planning. The classroom management and connecting with students were not surprising concerns given how Lynn described herself (i.e., "on the quiet side" and "not a great first impression kind of person"), the differences between her experiences and those of her students, and her apparent reticence to talk with the students she would be teaching. "Getting ready for class everyday" appeared daunting because "for every day, we will need a lesson plan. . . . I am mostly nervous about just getting everything ready, making sure I have rehearsed a little bit so I know what I am talking about and that, you know, I can go about and face the day's challenges."

While Lynn wanted to be consistent with respect to classroom management, which meant following her cooperating teacher even if she did not have a "big bellowy voice," she said that she wanted to try some different teaching ideas and see how they worked. Recall that Lynn had described her co-op as "very much [a] lecture, worksheet, take notes type of person." She described herself, in contrast, as "kind of looking forward to using visuals and demonstrations and that sort of thing to see if, you know, liven it up. It would be interesting to see the reactions or, like, if they're crazy or if, you know, if they really get into it." Lynn also referred to a special education teacher's advice to come to class prepared with alternatives for students who are encountering difficulties. Perhaps thinking about such on-the-spot changes contributed to making planning seem intimidating.

Classroom management continued to be challenging for Lynn (see Chapter 2), even with her co-op's support, as did connecting with students. The differences between Lynn and her students were considerable and, like Ken, she showed little inclination to meet them on some middle ground or find a workable common one. Compared with Ken, Lynn seemed more aware of her personal limitations going into Field Experience and student-teaching and the influence of her own background and high school experiences. Still, she talked about the kind of person she is, not about the kind of person she might like to become.

In our second conversation, Lynn first said that difference and diversity are not "as big a deal [at Royalton High School] as they [apparently from the university] always want us to believe." She continued: "I mean, there is diversity, there are different people who act different, there are different learning styles, like, all that sort of thing, but it's there. I think you get some of it anywhere." A few minutes later, in response to our question about any problems she had encountered working with students whose backgrounds and experiences differed from hers, Lynn indicated that difference was a big deal to/for her:

> I am from a background where you do your work, you work hard, it's your responsibility, that's your thing. You take responsibility for what you're doing, do it, get it done. . . . [A] lot of [Royalton] students . . . don't bring pens and paper because they don't want to do work, and so it gets them out of it. And, uh, they don't want to do work in general or they aren't going to do their homework. . . . [T]hey just don't appear to care.

On the basis of her experience, Lynn interpreted her students' behavior as not wanting to do the work and not caring—in other words, as being lazy and/or unmotivated. She wanted them to be more like her: "to take notes, to stay on task, um, to follow rules, be responsible for themselves and their actions." The differences between her background and her students' generated substantial tensions for Lynn, which she tried to account for in non-racial terms.

Referring to Ruby Payne's highly popularized "hidden rules of class" (e.g., Payne, 1998) and version of "generational poverty culture," Lynn said that the ways students behave (e.g., fighting) are:

> Part of their culture, but it's not part of the school culture, so they feel that they are doing what's right, but if a teacher or someone in administration, if they see it, they are obviously going to say, "hey, you can't be doing that," but it is the most natural thing for the students to do based on their experience and their past.

Asked how she thought she would "deal with the kids coming in from that culture," Lynn responded:

> I am not completely sure. I am just going to keep refreshing myself with those papers [readings] that "OK, this is some of the things that they do and that it is important to that culture," um, and just try to keep those things in mind when I see them doing different things and different behaviors and all that sort of thing, so I don't start pinning it on the individual and saying, "oh well, he is lazy because he doesn't do his homework." You know, it's, it's probably very much a culture thing so it doesn't impact the individual student or my view of the student. I don't know, maybe ways to try to, uh, somehow get around it. Like to try, um, yes, I guess to try to get around the culture without interfering, hmmm, respecting their culture for what it is but trying to help them see that school has a different culture. Kind of something like that, where they need certain skills to survive . . . in school and [the] professional world, which are not in their own culture, but respecting what they have and what they know and their skills there.

Lynn seemed to latch on to Payne's idea of generational poverty and its culture "because it is a nice set culture to refer to" that enabled her to explain, if not justify, behavior that was different from her own without using racial language or appearing overtly racist.

In response to the interviewer's wondering what, if any, strengths Lynn saw coming out of the students' home cultures, Lynn described a father coming into the school office and challenging something about his daughter. She concluded, "when you have the family, because not all of them do, the family ties are very important."

Just a few minutes later in the same conversation, Lynn told us, "I think my mind has started blanking out on all of the diversity stuff. I am just like, 'OK, good, there is diversity, good, now back to biology' [laughing]." Both Ken and Lynn tended to laugh when they said something that might be seen as closed-minded or bigoted: It appeared to be their way of easing possible tension or embarrassment. Asked about equity at Royalton High School, Lynn returned to the sameness and consistency that she and her co-op wanted to see schoolwide with respect to rule enforcement for student misbehavior (see Chapter 2). "I mean when it boils down to it, everyone's a student and all the students have to follow the same rules, and I would hope that administration and teachers and security and all those people deal with different people the same way."

Despite Lynn's claim of "diversity overload," we asked about changes in her ideas and beliefs. "They have definitely changed," she said and gave several nonschool examples, including one about her mother:

> I was talking to my mom the other day, and I feel horrible saying this because it's my mom, 'cus "mom, how can you think that?" . . . [W]e were talking on the way home, I don't know how we got on it, but some of it was, like, it was "they [African Americans] sound so dumb and unintelligent." I am, like, "no, they don't sound dumb. It's a different culture, it's a generational poverty. It is a whole different set of things that they need to survive." I am much more open and accepting of different people and different cultures and, um, and I can stand up to my mom and tell her all of these things. I don't know if she, if any of it sunk in at all, like, she said, "it's really too bad that that's the way it is." It certainly is, but, um, I am much more accepting, and I won't say, "oh, that person sounds dumb." It's the culture that person has grown up with.

So, Lynn may have become more open and accepting of other people and cultures, but there is still a way to go. Apparently, she might still find that a working- or lower-class African American "sounds dumb," but she would attribute the apparent dumbness to the culture of generational poverty, not to the person or the racial group.

Another example that Lynn volunteered involved the dolls on display (around Christmas) at a major grocery store and in toy store ads: "all the dolls are white, and I just want to be, like, 'hey! Not everybody's white.' . . . I am all up in arms about all this stuff. . . . 'Why are all these people [in ads] white?' They should be different colors, different races."

Lynn ended our conversation prior to her beginning student-teaching with this excited statement:

> I love being at [Royalton]. I mean, as much as I am "oh my gosh, I have to teach there next semester, and I have to survive for eight weeks," I really like it. It is so much fun because the people have so much

energy even if it's not directed in the right areas. I mean, they just come in, and they have energy, and [laughing] they are running around the room, and it is fun seeing that people are different instead of, you know, always seeing the same thing—suburban middle-class white students, like, I have had enough of that. Now that is what I grew up with. I have seen that, so this is just a great opportunity to spend a lot of time getting to know a different group of people.

Note that Lynn emphasized surviving and enjoying her students, not teaching them. Like Ken, who referred to his students as "expressive" and "fun," Lynn is exoticizing young people who are different from her. Her middle-class white culture is normal. Royalton students are exotic others. Both prospective teachers might like their students personally or individually, but they are uncomfortable with teaching them in a class of 15 to 30 students.

Lynn acknowledged this individual-group distinction in our last conversation at the end of her student-teaching at Royalton: "they [students] are great people, they have great personalities, interests, hobbies, skills. It's just mixing them in and putting them in a class" that is a problem. She returned to what I call her "culture as culprit" theme in explaining why Royalton students are not always getting the education they have a right to: "part of it is because of their culture, the way they grow up [referring to black students' avoiding charges of "acting white"]. . . . I am not really blaming them. It's just the way it is, and I don't know how you undo it." Another "part of it" may well be low expectations on the part of teachers and other school personnel. Lynn, however, is blaming the victims via their "culture," and seems to have both absolved herself of any responsibility and given up on trying to connect with them.

For someone who "had never heard good things about city schools," who had only once before "ever been put in with a group of people where I am one of the minority," and who apparently was not "aware of poverty" beyond abstract statistics, Lynn can be seen to have become more open to and accepting of difference, as she claims. Her apparent lifesaver, a "culture" of generational poverty à la Ruby Payne, however, seems to serve as a set of blinders or a roadblock to further learning that might result in more open and constructive engagement with diversity.

At the end of our last conversation, Lynn revealed that teaching was not her first career choice. Her "passion," she said, is interpretation and informal education, like being a naturalist at a state or national park. She was very pleased, however, at having survived student-teaching at Royalton High School and having "tons of good [class] periods, not necessarily every whole day."

I'm happy I'm alive, and I am happy I'm through it. . . . Not because I was worried about being killed because of violence, just like, "I am done. I did it. Holy cow, I made it." Like that sort of alive. I knew going into it I probably wasn't cut out for an urban situation just because . . . it takes a special person to work in an urban setting and really be effective there, and I don't think I'm a special person in that way.

Once again, Lynn retreats to the kind of person she is/is not, and absolves herself of responsibility for constructively engaging student difference and diversity.

Lynn's second student-teaching placement, at a suburban middle school, was reportedly more successful. I understand that she completed her master's degree at the university during the following year and accepted a teaching position on the East Coast for the fall of 2007.

CONCLUSIONS

Both prospective teachers praised Nolan as a cooperating teacher, especially his advice and assistance with classroom management (Lynn) or control (Ken), even though they continued to have problems. Instructionally, Nolan was more likely to provide feedback than direction in advance. At times in our conversations, both PTs seemed to be echoing Nolan's complaints about school and district policies and administrators. Lynn acknowledged Nolan's influence and "going along" as appropriate to her view of the student-teacher role: "I smile during the faculty meetings when everybody's clapping, and I clap along with them—I just pretend. I am also not in a place where I can really say or do anything about it. As a student-teacher I just have to follow along and hear what my CT says and what he thinks."

Although her co-op influenced her, Lynn found some of his assertions too extreme:

Oh, sure it [her co-op's opinion] probably did [influence her], because I spent so much time with him and his friends that I think it had to, but I think in a lot of cases he had good points, and he wasn't just, like, being vindictive. But, um, sometimes I think he also went over the top. Like administration would do one little thing, and they would be in an uproar, like, "oh, I don't like this. I don't like this. . . . Oh, we might have to talk to the union about it."

She presented herself as "just trying to get along . . . to blend in and be friendly."

Ken, in contrast, did not evidence such recognition. Recall also that he did not recount receiving many messages about the school, the students, or "how we do things here." Like Rupert, he was largely "out of the loop" (see Chapter 3).

These cases of Lynn and Ken illustrate the interaction or mix of individual and institutional influences that shape how prospective teachers engage difference and diversity. Here, institutional influences appear primarily in the person of their cooperating teacher, Nolan, and his friends, who comprise one of the distinctly negative teacher groups at Royalton High School. Individual influences are apparent as well. Personally, Lynn is more sociable (at times even effusive, at least with project staff) and appears to go along, whereas Ken seems to be more of a loner or outsider and perhaps more needy. In terms of connecting with students, both had some small successes and larger difficulties in part because of their expectation that the way they were brought up should be the day-to-day standard for their students.

Ken seemed distressed by the realization that even the white students at Royalton were not like him. He was at a loss about coping with the differences, while Lynn embraced Ruby Payne's ideas about generational poverty and working-class culture to explain Royalton students' behavior that was at odds with her own. Lynn's cultural difference response at times seemed to merge with a cultural deficit position and, thus, came closer to Ken's talk of different levels. In any event, Lynn and Ken saw themselves as being worlds apart from their students. If there was to be change, it should come from the students, even if that was unlikely. Their presumption was that the students should take responsibility for becoming more like them; if they did not do so, then Lynn and Ken (in their minds) were not at fault.

Unlike the colorblindness of Radical Individualism, the Worlds Apart stance maintains an awareness of race or color difference (but not necessarily diversity), and may even involve an exaggeration of the proportion of students of color in a classroom or school. As in the cases here, it also can incorporate social-class differences (e.g., in language use or behavior) and differences in perceived student ability and/or motivation to learn. Not unlike Kirk, who entered Charter School largely ignorant and fearful of people unlike himself, Ken and Lynn saw themselves and their students as coming from different worlds. Where Kirk changed his ideas and beliefs somewhat as he got to know his students, Ken and Lynn did not. They maintained their distance, worlds apart.

The racism of "Worlds Apart" may be passive (Tatum, 1997) or dysconscious (King, 1991), or simply unacknowledged and indirect. Although it may be the result of isolation and ignorance rather than malevolence, it is not without negative effects on students of color (e.g., Irvine, 2003; Marx, 2006). The same is true for classism and other bases for social hierarchy and "othering." Deficit thinking and low expectations, for example, whether racially or culturally based, affect relationships with students as well as what and how we try to teach them. By distancing ourselves from our students rather than trying to connect with them, teachers are more likely to underestimate or otherwise misjudge student abilities, pass class time rather than use it productively, and then criticize students for being apathetic or disruptive.

While Radical Individualism maintains a focus on getting to know students and on academic learning, even if narrowly construed, Worlds Apart eschews connecting with students and anything more than bare-bones teaching for getting by, a kind of "defensive teaching" first described by McNeil (1986). In McNeil's account, based on her study of four Midwestern high schools, some teachers simplified the subject matter and otherwise limited the academic demands placed on students (e.g., little or no homework; few, if any, writing assignments) in exchange for their cooperation in class. Teachers, according to McNeil:

> choose to simplify content and reduce demands on students in return for classroom order and minimal student compliance on assignments. . . . [T]hey teach "defensively," choosing methods of presentation and evaluation that they hope will make their workload more efficient and create as little student resistance as possible. (1986, p. 158)

Defensive methods or techniques include (1) fragmentation, "the reduction of any topic to fragments or disjointed pieces of information" (p. 167), such as lists of terms to define; (2) mystification or treating a complex topic such as gravity superficially, as important but unknowable; (3) omission, usually of controversial topics or points of view such as evolution; and (4) a more general simplification to circumvent a perceived lack of student interest or abilities. Here, teachers seek "students' compliance on a lesson by promising that it will not be difficult and will not go into any depth" (p. 174). Defensive teaching thus minimizes both teaching and student learning.

Defensive teaching, modeled here by co-op Nolan and eventually adopted by Ken and Lynn, despite their initial intentions to do more, has varied and sometimes multiple causes. It is seen to ease classroom management or concerns about order (although there is evidence and argument to support just the opposite) and to be efficient in terms of teacher time and effort. In addition, defensive teaching both reflects and contributes to low expectations for students. Because students are seen as lacking

background knowledge or skills for more engaging activities and meaningful learning, as well as appropriate behavior, they are given more structured, usually rote, individual assignments that engender student boredom,
not completing work, and failing tests, and, thus, reinforcing the teacher's
low expectations for them. It is an unfortunately common illustration of
the self-fulfilling prophecy in action.

At least two implications for teacher education are painfully obvious.
One is to help prospective and newer teachers recognize and interrupt the
twin dead ends of defensive teaching and the self-fulfilling prophecy of
low expectations. Both are self-deceptive traps, trapping both teachers and
students in a lose-lose situation of unsatisfying teacher-student relations
and minimal student learning. They do, however, serve to maintain the
status quo within and outside schools, including middle-class white privilege. A second implication is to exercise caution so that the readings we
assign, the activities we employ, and the discussions we encourage in
teacher education do not serve to entrench difference and distance. Lynn's
uncritical use of a Ruby Payne reading about generational poverty and its
"culture," for example, vividly illustrates such problems. It also reminds
us of the appeal of anecdotal accounts or personal stories, which too often
is stronger than the weight of systematically obtained and relatively im-
personal evidence.

Now, I turn to much more productive responses to student difference
and diversity from prospective teachers in our project and teachers elsewhere. They represent a range of ways to bridge different worlds.

6

Bridging Different Worlds

Bridging Different Worlds is the most common and variable approach to engaging student difference and diversity among the more successful prospective teachers we followed, as well as among outstanding newer and experienced teachers studied by myself and others (e.g., Ladson-Billings, 1994; Sleeter, 2005). For prospective and newer teachers, this bridging doesn't just happen or happen as easily as may appear to be the case for experienced teachers. The vignettes and cases presented here show teachers struggling to connect with their students, to find some common or neutral ground both personally and academically, and to communicate effectively. At least to some extent, that usually meant learning one another's language, even when that language is English. It means that the teachers move into previously unfamiliar territory, just as they are asking their students to do. They are not staying put, demanding that their students take all the risks and do all the work. The various forms of bridging and accommodation illustrated here offer hope for constructive engagement with student difference and diversity that brings meaningful student learning and teacher satisfaction.

Included within Bridging Different Worlds is a variant that I call "Culture Shock and Accommodation," which also attempts to communicate and connect with students who are different from oneself—after an initial period of anxiety and uncertainty. Ken and Lynn, in contrast, stopped short of accommodation (see Chapter 5). Instead of maintaining a self-protective distance (which usually turns out not to be helpful at all), with Culture Shock and Accommodation, PTs seek a personal or personalized connection with students, both to allay their fears and to open doors to academic teaching and learning. Successful prospective and newer teachers who are more comfortable with student difference and diversity initially tend to connect with students both personally and academically, usually with an academic emphasis. If Worlds Apart (see Chapter 5) is characterized by distance, Bridging Different Worlds is characterized by teachers and students connecting with one another, as well as with academic and experiential knowledge, via multiple bridges with several access lanes in each direction.

Three pairs of prospective teachers are presented here, representing various points along a continuum from Culture Shock and Accommodation to Bridging Different Worlds. Cases of other successful newer and experienced teachers are included as well. The first pair of PTs, Mark and Jaclyn, both in social studies, represent Culture Shock and Accommodation. Another example is provided by Fred, an experienced English teacher who moved from a suburban parochial school to a city school. The second pair, Cora in science and Amanda in English, represent a middle point, while the third pair, Kate in science and Malcolm in social studies, seemed most comfortable with student diversity and began building bridges soon after they arrived at Royalton High School. Additional examples are provided by teachers elsewhere. Amanda, Kate, and Malcolm all had prior paid or volunteer experience working with people different from themselves, and did not demonstrate unease about engaging students of different racial/ethnic groups or religious beliefs. Although such experience is no guarantee of openness, understanding, and respect, there was a positive association in these three cases. The most space is given to Amanda and Cora here, so readers can "see" and learn from their struggles and bridging efforts. Not only did they say more than many of the prospective teachers we followed, but I suspect that they "speak" to many other new teachers as well.

The bridge-building described here is substantial but incomplete. These teachers illustrate possibilities or work in progress that is attainable by others.

CULTURE SHOCK AND ACCOMMODATION

Mark and Jaclyn worked with different social studies cooperating teachers, Mark in year 1 of the project and Jaclyn in year 2. As you might recall (from Chapters 2 and 3), they were among the prospective teachers who were most openly apprehensive about being placed at an urban school. Unlike Ken and Lynn, however, they made major efforts to remain open-minded and learn from their experiences at Royalton High School. Jaclyn and Mark also had a strong desire to succeed, not merely survive. They were supported by positive co-ops who tended not to hang out with negative teachers in a relatively cohesive and supportive department. In their cases, the mix of individual and institutional influences worked to the advantage of all those involved.

Jaclyn: Turnabout

For whatever reasons, Jaclyn never thought that she would be placed at an urban school for Field Experience or student-teaching. She described herself as "really not familiar" with racial/ethnic difference and diversity or with being in the minority as a white person. She was surprised that the teacher education program "pushed" diversity (e.g., "think about this, reflect on that") and did not think that she would have to deal with it so much. Jaclyn said that her parents raised her "to be open to things," and diversity had not been an issue growing up or traveling (e.g., on a semester abroad in Europe). Royalton High School was simply more different and diverse than anything she had encountered previously.

A student fight near the beginning of the school year (between two female students, seriously injuring a teacher who tried to intervene and stop it) and several student fights later on also rattled Jaclyn, leading her to "question sometimes the security of it [student-teaching at Royalton]." She characterized the situation as stressful and worrying to teachers, requiring continual awareness and monitoring, not simply teaching. It appeared that at least some of Jaclyn's concerns were fed by family and/or friends. (Representatives of the university teacher education program did meet with Royalton representatives at the school in January prior to the beginning of student-teaching and came away satisfied that Royalton was safe for student-teachers.) Jaclyn's sense of isolation and threat also might be due in part to the differences between her situation as she saw it at Royalton and the accounts of PTs at other schools with whom she talked. An example she offered was that "for all of my other friends, it is more of a teaching experience, and it is not important that they get to know the students as well."

Also challenging Jaclyn's prior experience was encountering loud, assertive female students: "the girls seem to have a really strong demeanor about them" that Jaclyn associated with boys' behavior:

> I hear them yelling at the boys in the hallway. They don't seem to be very willing to submit to anything around them. Like, um, they just won't have it, they're just going to say and do what they want, whereas experiences that I've had, it is usually the males that are, like, that loud and obnoxious and making problems in the back of the classroom. . . . They [girls] will be the first to walk out of class if they disagree with the teacher. I have really never experienced that before or seen it. It's usually, I don't know, maybe my situations weren't as diverse, but I just, I usually picture the males as storming out of the classroom and just being, like, "that teacher's a bitch" whereas it's the

girls that do it more at [Royalton]. . . . I feel like they feel like they have to be in order to achieve some sort of, I don't know, status in school or among their peers to make it known that they are people too and . . . that they cannot be pushed around.

For Jaclyn, especially early on:

things at [Royalton] are complicated. Um, it doesn't necessarily have to be a bad complicated, just for me as a future student-teacher, um, there are things that I've had to think about that I've never had to think about before . . . but it is important to, and I am having to do it now [laughing].

Trying to keep an open mind and learning from the experience at Royalton High School made a tremendous difference for Jaclyn. She noted that she learned a lot from observing a range of teachers and how students reacted to them. Her attitude changed during student-teaching as she successfully connected with her students personally and academically and came to feel like part of the Royalton family. Recall Jaclyn looking back and saying, "I decided before I went there, I wasn't happy, but then, right before I got there, I just decided to just completely erase my mind of everything. . . . I really tried to grow within myself and find something I could learn from."

Other than initial discomfort with her own minority status, Jaclyn said that she did not see diversity as an issue at Royalton and that it "just doesn't need to be addressed." By this, she meant, like Amanda and Cora, to be presented in the next section, that diversity was not divisive or a source of tension as she apparently had expected. Even the student fights were within racial/ethnic groupings.

Difference and diversity were an issue for Jaclyn and a key part of her efforts to communicate and connect with her students personally, which she cited as her greatest challenge at Royalton. "Connecting with students in positive ways," Jaclyn said, was not only a strong message at Royalton from teachers and administrators, but also one that she heard before she arrived: "It's the most important thing to do with the students if you plan on being successful. You had to connect with them. If you didn't, you lost them, there's just nothing. You had to connect with the students, and . . . I tried many different things." Recall (see Chapter 2) her efforts to learn and use students' names, to create a kind of community in her classroom, to be in the hallway near the classroom door between classes and talk with students individually. Additional examples she offered included "using more authentic stuff in the classroom" such as journals and collages as "little ways that I can, um, understand them, and they can share a little bit of themselves with me."

Verbal communication with students also was a major concern initially, specifically understanding their dialects, accents, and slang. She hoped that students would not brush her off when she asked them to repeat, clarify, or slow down because she wanted to understand what they were saying. Most students responded positively to her sincerity.

In addition to her own determination, effort, and a supportive co-op, coming to feel like a member of the Royalton family made a substantial difference for Jaclyn. It provided a virtual life raft of reassurance and encouragement to venture beyond her previous limits of experience and understanding. She told me:

> So, even though they have their problems, they do pull together, and you can see that in the school. . . . I think that the teachers there feel that if they form a bond together and if they hold strong, that their students will see that and almost, um, conform to it in a way and stick together themselves as having pride in their school and, um, just making positive things happen rather than looking at the negative things. . . . I did! I really did [feel part of a family atmosphere]. And that's probably why I fell in love with the place. They, like, pull you in to this family [laughs], and it makes you really feel great about what you're doing there, and especially the department, the social studies department I was in, they, I think more than some of the other departments there, they met more and talked to each other more, and shared more information. I think, this was the vibe I got from the school.

Jaclyn came to selectively accept and adopt the constructive messages she received at Royalton, attributing any teacher negativity to "those bad days."

Looking back on what turned out to be a very successful student-teaching experience at Royalton High School, Jaclyn commented, "I learned so much more than I thought I would, and I had such a better experience, a better experience than I ever was expecting, that it really blows my mind every time I think about it." She continued:

> it's hard to hear people talk about the school now, because I'm defensive about it. I'm, like, "no, it's a good school, you know, the teachers are great, the students want to learn" . . . probably half of them . . . it really changed my view of teaching in urban, city school districts.

Mark: More Than Luck

Mark's feeling of culture shock when he was assigned to and then arrived at Royalton High School was more matter-of-fact than Jaclyn's, and he did not seem concerned about safety. Coming from a very white suburb and high school, he had no prior experience with a city school or urban students. Being "scared" was a product of personal unfamiliarity with city schools and students and hearing the negative messages about them. Mark said that he "really didn't know what to expect . . . and I, I wasn't pretending that I, I was gonna know. . . . I just had to, like, see it for myself." Initially, like several other prospective teachers, Mark overestimated the proportion of African American students at Royalton. He was also fascinated by the presence in one of his classes of a student from Somalia and another from Vietnam.

Seemingly more than (or more consciously than) most of the prospective teachers in the two cohorts we followed at Royalton, Mark took advantage of the available support system, including his cooperating teacher and other teachers in the department, his university supervisor-mentor, and other PTs at Royalton. Referring to the cohort of PTs, Mark said, "we took that initial step to be friendly with one another, get to know each other, and then went on to help one another out." He gave an example of sharing ideas and feedback with another social studies PT, Malcolm, "'cus we're both, like, 'OK, how are we going to make this interesting?' Um, I believe that was huge." Mark liked his co-op and came to greatly admire and appreciate him as well as learn from him.

Mark's major concerns initially were connecting with students personally and classroom management, both of which can be seen to reflect his apprehensions about a diverse urban school. As described earlier (see Chapters 2 and 3), Mark soon modified his thinking to emphasize making the subject matter (U.S. history and government) relevant in order to interest students and making his instruction active and challenging to involve them. He was working to relate to students academically as well as personally, and found that classroom management followed from those efforts. Mark related an early experience at Royalton that helped him realize that teaching well is not simply telling:

> my first time I taught in front of the students, I talked a lot. And, um, my teacher said, you know, "You can't get away with that in here [unclear]. You're gonna be tired, and you're gonna bore the students, and it doesn't matter, you can have the best lesson or whatever, but you gotta keep them involved. And so you gotta draw things from the students, and so you have to ask them questions." And I found that, 'cause I taught this lesson for three different periods, is that as I went on and asked more of the students, they got more involved.

This experience appeared to have made an impression on Mark, and he worked to involve students in meaningful learning and critical thinking.

Approximately one-third of the prospective teachers at Royalton talked about, and appeared to act on, higher expectations for students that included critical thinking (Mark, Cora, Kate, Malcolm). Mark put it this way:

> students are more responsive when you ask them to think . . . the students can think, you know, it doesn't matter where they're from or whatever . . . you just have to give them that push to think.

Critical thinking was related to Mark's insistence on high expectations. He described himself as "one of those crazy people who think you can actually make a difference with people" in contrast to "a lot of people [who] just assume that city schools, city kids are doomed to fail." If you set high expectations for students, Mark said, "they will meet them . . . you know, don't tell them they can't do anything. . . . I believe they will rise to whatever expectations you give them."

Efforts to actively involve students who usually just sat silently in class illustrates Mark's beliefs:

> [When] I was observing, I saw kids that usually don't talk, and I tried to make sure that my goal was to, you know, get them to express their opinions or something. And so, like, when it came down to . . . what we were comparing, maybe like getting involved with foreign affairs or something like that, I asked, you know, I kept asking, like the kids that didn't talk before, you know, "What do you think? You got an opinion?" and they would actually, like, speak and express their opinion where they had never talked before.

Expressing opinions can be seen as a first step to more substantive participation.

Mark's emphasis on high expectations also connected with his belief that teachers should take students' ethnic or racial background into account, but should not make it the main focus of their teaching and get sidetracked by "overthinking." Knowing your students was necessary for making things relevant and interesting so students would learn, not an end in itself.

Among the examples of making past/present comparisons and relating U.S. history to students' lives that Mark noted were Pearl Harbor and *Plessy* v. *Ferguson* (the 1896 Supreme Court decision that allowed "separate but equal" public facilities for blacks and whites):

> Depending on the certain event, like, it's easier to compare Pearl Harbor to 9/11 because it is two different incidents where we were

attacked. But, like social issues and stuff, you have to really, like, dig deep down, like, um, but it is really focusing on the student. Like, what's really going on in the student's life. And then seeing how in any way is this similar to, um, an event in history. So, like, I think the best example would be, like, *Plessy* versus *Ferguson*, separate but equal. So, I am thinking, like, okay, well, what do the students know, and I might ask them, and I ask them to write [about] a time when they felt discriminated against or that they thought they weren't equal in some way and then, like, relate to how the *Plessy* versus *Ferguson* kind of supported that idea. And, you know, they were able to understand that better.

Summing up his experience connecting with students, Mark claimed "for one reason or another, it just worked out, you know . . . I don't know, it just came like nature. It just happened. There is no real way to explain it. . . . I lucked out big time."

My sense is that Mark is being way too modest in attributing his success in relating to students to "luck." From recognizing potential problems (stemming from different backgrounds and experiences), to careful classroom observation and learning from his students, to joking with students (sometimes at his own expense), to establishing rules and academic expectations, to connecting past and present as well as historical events to students' lives, to showing that he cared about students by being responsive to their questions and listening to their relevant stories, to pushing his students and challenging them to think critically (which communicates higher expectations), to using different strategies to reach more students, Mark was doing quite a bit to foster good relationships with students and their meaningful academic learning.

An example of how far Mark had moved in bridging different worlds is his joking with students about white guys playing basketball. He told me:

we were talking about basketball, and then I played basketball with them, and the kids were, like, the kids were all shocked, and they were like "you play basketball?" and I would joke with them "oh, it is because I am white," and they thought it was the funniest thing.

Mark became an energetic supporter of Royalton and urban students, concluding that he would rather teach there than in the suburbs. "I really want to really help students out and in this case people are giving up on them. . . . [T]here are a lot of bright kids in there, but, you know, they might not be given the chance that they should." Anyone could teach if every student was well behaved, loved the subject, and wanted to learn, Mark said.

Fred: Starting Over

Even more experienced teachers can undergo culture shock and face the challenges of accommodation to student difference and diversity. Fred provides a compelling example. He had taught English for several years, both as a permanent substitute in a selective-admission city high school and in a suburban parochial school with 5th and 6th graders. He then left teaching for a year to make some money as a consultant with a company that trained teachers to use technology. Fred said that he missed the students, so when the city school district called and offered him a regular position with full pay and benefits, he came back home. The position was teaching 8th-grade English in a recently remodeled, grade 3–8 Urban Academy not far from Royalton High School. Fred was in his third year at Middle Academy when I met him in 2001. He agreed to be interviewed and invited me to visit his classes.

Fred described his first year at Middle Academy as disastrous. His high expectations were dashed; every day was disappointing. His previous approach just was not working with less affluent students, many of whom were Hispanic and African American. Fred said that at first he blamed his students, then himself, and he frequently thought seriously about quitting because he did not know what else to do. During the summer after his first year at Middle Academy, Fred began to read about other teachers' experiences with "inner-city kids," and what he learned led to major changes in both his relationships with students and his teaching. He came around, he told me, to see the need to respect his students and to learn more about them in order to gain their respect and teach them successfully. He demonstrated that he cared about them, for example, by listening to them, hearing them out, and taking them seriously. Fred also communicated confidence that his students could do the work and acknowledged when their work was well done.

His teaching was more flexible now, he said, adjusting to students' moods and geared toward their lives and interests. Writing assignments, for example, are more often thematic and provide options for students. He has diversified his literature selections to include Langston Hughes' poetry, Maya Angelou's poetry and excerpts from other writing, Lorraine Hansberry's *Raisin in the Sun*, Richard Wright's "Not Poor, Just Broke," James Baldwin's letter to his nephew, selections from Toni Morrison, and Sandra Cisneros's *House on Mango Street*. The class reads a book and does a project every few weeks now.

The book project I observed was a "Vignette Style (Paperless) Writing Project" with Fred's 8th-grade transitional English class of 11 students who have done well in the bilingual Spanish-English program but are judged to still need some language support. It was inspired, Fred said, by Greg Michie's experiences as a new teacher in Chicago, recounted in *Holler If You Hear Me* (1999). They had read *House on Mango Street* and were working in the computer lab composing three vignettes about their own lives using some of Cisneros's literary techniques (e.g., metaphor, personification, imagery). The students I observed were involved in authentic writing and revision. They seemed to know what to do, and they got to work, asking each other or Fred for assistance as needed. Before one class I observed, Fred went down to the in-school detention room to retrieve a student he thought would be better off in class. The boy came in and sat down at a computer, took a folded sheet of paper with some writing on it out of his jeans pocket, and began typing. He had written two vignettes at home and was now typing them up. There was no doubt that the students were involved in the project. According to Nancy, a student whose writing about the experience was quoted in the district's bilingual/ESL newsletter, "This book is a different type of book. I can relate to it. . . . Sandra Cisneros . . . has captivated me and has opened my heart like the sun comes up shining."

Later, Fred told me that teachers "need to change because times have changed" and "kids have changed," too. This was only his second year with the transitional bilingual class. Last year was difficult, he said, because he did not know what to do and did not speak Spanish. Fred had insisted that the students use only English, and there were problems with that. Now, he proudly described students writing in English or in Spanish to be translated into English later, but keeping some Spanish words or phrases for "flavor." Accommodation and bridge-building are continuing processes, as Fred's experiences well illustrate.

Fred's accommodation and bridge-building provide exemplars of culturally responsive teaching. In selecting authors from his students' racial/ethnic/cultural backgrounds who "speak to" the students' experiences, he is both reaching out and drawing in. There are not simply token or symbolic author choices. There is less evidence of such robust responsiveness in Mark's and especially Jaclyn's teaching, perhaps because of the differences in subject area (U.S. and global history versus English), role (student versus regular teacher), knowledge, and experience, as well as individual inclination. Cultural responsiveness was quite evident, however, in their continuing efforts to connect with students, individually and collectively, personally and academically.

Fred, Jaclyn, and Mark all display what has been called resilience, usually in reference to students who are able to bounce back from, deflect, or overcome difficult circumstances. In these cases, it is the teachers who display resilience. They work hard and successfully to adjust to change and challenges. From another perspective, they can be seen to hold high expectations for themselves and to strive to meet them. Accommodation and bridge-building are not for slackers.

BUILDING BRIDGES FROM DIFFERENT ACCESS ROUTES

Amanda, a prospective English teacher in the first year of our project, and Cora, a prospective science teacher in the second year, came to Royalton High School from different backgrounds and by different routes. Once there, however, despite very dissimilar cooperating teachers, they shared several noteworthy commonalities in their approach to student difference and diversity, including the nature of changes in their beliefs about how difference matters.

Amanda was a self-described "nontraditional student" at the university, in her late twenties (about 6 years older than the other prospective teachers we followed) and married with a young child. Cora was younger and single. She described growing up in a single-parent family, living in largely white rural areas, and being "on welfare," including free school lunches, for a while. In contrast, Amanda grew up in a family with two parents (her father divorced and remarried several times) in an affluent suburb, and attended a predominantly white, high-status high school. With some experience with people different from herself during prior work experiences, Amanda did not appear apprehensive about Royalton High School and its students. She did find that dealing constructively with student difference and diversity was more complex and challenging than she had anticipated, and she worked quite hard to meet the challenges. For example, looking back on her experience at Royalton, Amanda said:

> I wasn't expecting for diversity to be an issue at all. Like, I have worked in [unintelligible] places, I have worked with people who are different. . . . I just never thought it would be something I would take into consideration. I thought for me it was, like, I knew you [unintelligible] respectful of different cultural and things like that, but I never realized how much of an actual challenge it is in the classroom. That different cultures, like, the different opinions, the different response to the same literature . . . I had to explain because most of my students weren't Catholic, they didn't understand what Romeo and Juliet [unintelligible] in when they got married and, like, the picture in the book [of Romeo and Juliet kneeling, indicating that they were in church]. . . . I just had to be more aware of, like, what cultural norms were. And I guess I didn't expect that to ever be, like, an issue. And what people's frame of reference was. And how much it mattered to them. I mean, we

watched, like, the new Romeo and Juliet and because they were so excited 'cus there was someone in it that was black . . . and that meant something to them.

Initially, Amanda thought of difference and diversity rather superficially in terms of respect or of divisiveness and interpersonal or intergroup conflict. She had not previously considered that it would matter very much in terms of subject-matter content or the effective communication that is essential to successful teaching and learning.

Diversity was relatively new for Cora. She said that although there was a socioeconomic range of students at her high school, it was predominantly white, as was the state college that she attended as an undergraduate. The university was her first experience with both a large school and considerable diversity, and she did not know what to expect at Royalton High School. Then, negative external messages about urban schools, including some from the university, generated apprehension: "They kind of influenced me, like, a little bit when I first walked in. I was a little nervous." Sources of negative messages from the university included other students, a video shown in a sociology of education class, and an instructor who repeated media reports about fights at Royalton. Cora related:

> She asked us all, "Where are you going for your Field Experience?" "Oh, [Royalton] High School." And she just looked at me, she's like, "That should be interesting," and I was like, "What do you mean by that?" and she told me about some, like, past stories. . . . So, at first I was, like, "Oh man, what have I gotten myself into?"

However, Cora told us, once she was out at Royalton "and sat through the classes and things like that," her apprehension faded.

> I mean it is just a school like any other. I mean it's got its problems. I mean I am not afraid to walk the halls, I am not afraid to sit in classrooms, I am not afraid to interact with the students. It was a lot different from the initial impression I had when I was walking in . . . just seeing the students and interacting with them. They're just high school kids, just trying to get through high school and get on with their lives or whatever. I mean, obviously, they come from not so great an area, which kind of affects them, and they bring that [poverty, gangs, violence] into school sometimes. But, generally, they are just people, so I didn't think I had anything to be afraid of really.

From there, Cora worked to "spark their interests" and "find some way to connect with the students."

A last difference to be noted here is the cooperating teachers with whom Amanda and Cora worked. Amanda's co-op was a younger, black female who Amanda described as holding high expectations for students and being her role model:

> [She] expected them to understand things, and she really tried to expose them to a lot of things. . . . [S]he didn't really give up. Where I saw other teachers, like, give up, she really stuck with what she wanted to teach and what she thought was important. And it definitely, you saw students, like, that it reached. . . . I think that her perseverance really, she never, like, kinda gave in to that temptation to, uh, to assign them bookwork everyday. So, like everyday she still had activities and all sorts of stuff, and I think that was really good, that was a good kind of message for me. . . . I think that she kind of really instilled in me, like, to force them to do things outside their comfort zones.

And Amanda learned to "block out the negative voices" from other teachers.

Cora's co-op was a middle-aged white female who Cora described as "kind of burnt out" about the students and teaching, but who gave Cora leeway to try out different teaching strategies. Later, Cora reflected, "I guess that works also to sort of kick up my enthusiasm too, 'cause I don't want to be like that, you know. I want to be excited, so I guess that sort of helps out, like, even seeing the negative sort of reinforces what I want to do."

Amanda and Cora were the only two prospective teachers to voice concerns about Royalton students distancing or rejecting them as white outsiders. More common was the observation that it was unusual and uncomfortable to be in the minority as a white person. Their concerns were more a feeling than anything specific or tangible, other than Amanda's cooperating teacher being black and the majority of their students being African American and Hispanic. (During year one, whites slightly outnumbered Hispanics; the following year saw the reverse.) Amanda put it this way:

> [M]ost of my students were African American or Hispanic, and I was white, so they thought that I couldn't possibly understand them. Um, my cooperating teacher was African American, so I think that they almost kind of, I thought at the beginning, it was just like I felt, like, I was intruding on this safe place, 'cus there are so few teachers that aren't white, even in urban settings. . . . Sometimes I felt like I was intruding, and I couldn't quite talk to them in the same way.

Initially, Cora said that she was concerned about being written off as "that white girl" before she and her students got to know one another personally. She told us:

> Like in general, they're pretty nice to me, but I know, I can tell, I can almost sense that they're just like "eh, white girl coming to teach the poor students," you know, things like that. So, hopefully I can work to, you know, if not totally eliminate the stereotype obviously, but at least make it better, like a better relationship between student and teacher. I feel like the students sort of distance themselves from the teachers 'cause the teachers don't understand them or think something like that.

Amanda and Cora's concerns apparently dissipated as they came to know and work with Royalton students; neither mentioned them again. Their language suggests that the perceived problem was largely, if not entirely, in their minds. What is important to *Diversity and the New Teacher* is that Amanda and Cora sought to know, accept, and be accepted by their students. They did not give in or give up.

Overall, Amanda and Cora seemed self-confident in a matter-of-fact way. They were open and willing to learn what they thought would help them become successful teachers, and both PTs made constructive changes in their understanding of and responses to student difference and diversity. At the same time, they continued to experience tensions between white, middle-class school expectations and their increasing understanding of students coming from different situations.

Amanda: Making It Matter

Recall (from Chapters 2 and 3) that Amanda saw her major challenges at Royalton as connecting with students academically and fostering student engagement, which she described as "making it matter to them." Making it matter was a continuing struggle, given all that was going on in her students' lives in and outside school. Amanda kept trying to connect English (e.g., a play or poem, writing an essay) to students' interests and what was happening in the world. She also worked to show them "how important in life being able to communicate is."

As she moved toward a deeper understanding of difference and diversity, Amanda was better equipped to engage her students in academic learning. She began from what has been called a "pizza and polka" version of multiculturalism. Amanda described herself and the changes in her thinking this way:

Um, I think I was probably more of the dress up in costumes, have nice food, and read some poetry [laughs] night as a multicultural event when I started 'cause that's what I'd been exposed to. Even, I went to [state college], and, you know, even going there, which was very diverse, my program wasn't very diverse. You know, we celebrated Black History Month and Women's History Month, and it was very isolated and I think that, I think the biggest thing I've learned is that it, it's harder than it seems but it can be done. But you really have to work to make it a part of what you're doing. And to really, I don't know, it's hard to say, like, to think about it but not think about it all the time, to focus on making it just part of what you do and not like an aside, you know, an aside to what you're doing. And I think, like, for me, that's what I've learned the challenge is, to integrate it without making it separate. So, you have to, like, focus on it [laughs], focus on not focusing on it almost, if that makes any sense. But I think to me, that's really what I've learned is that, to make it really work, it needs to just be what you do and not be, like, forced or, or an isolated event.

While Amanda did not use the language of inclusive curriculum or culturally relevant teaching, that seemed to be what she was describing when she talked about incorporating varied cultural experiences and perspectives as well as authors, "making it just part of what you do," rather than an aside or add-on. Getting there was a struggle given her starting point and the limited resources at Royalton.

Amanda initially described Royalton as having "a huge racial diversity" and seemed surprised that students from different groups mixed and that there was little evidence of intergroup tension or conflict. She had expected racial/ethnic diversity to be divisive. In her words:

I've noticed a lot of [sigh], of students sort of sticking to their, like, their own races in some ways, but I have lunch duty, and it's amazing how many tables I see that do have mixes. And I know a lot of times that, that you don't really see that. So I, I don't, I don't see it as being a huge conflict . . . they seem to really meld well, um, I think what part of town you're from is more important there [laughs].

She continued:

I think because the, the school knows it's so diverse, it really kind of, it embraces it in some ways. Again, like it has that very Christian overtone [laughs]. Um, but I think because it's just so diverse . . . it's like 54% African American and then the rest of it's sort of split up. Um

[5-second pause, approximately], I guess I've learned that in some ways how it can, like, work. Like, they seem to be very integrated and there doesn't seem to be, like, you know . . . when you tell the kids to work in the groups, it doesn't seem to be like all of the white kids work together and all of the, you know, maybe, Hispanic kids work together, they definitely seem to be integrated somewhat.

From seeing students of different racial groups working together voluntarily and sitting together (also voluntarily) in the cafeteria at Royalton, Amanda concluded that "I think in some ways I've almost learned it's [diversity] not as big of a deal, at least there, as I thought it would be." Neither were the Christmas tree, decorations, and study of Christmas literature in some English classes that surprised and disturbed Amanda.

At this point (the end of Field Experience and just prior to student-teaching), Amanda decided "almost not to worry about it [diversity] as much as I thought I would and to really look at students individually. . . . I think it's [diversity] always, like, in the back of my mind because I don't wanna come off as being insensitive, so I do try to think about it. . . . I think that basically I learned just not to assume anything." After a rambling story about mistakenly calling a student by an Americanized version of his Middle Eastern name (she had misheard it), and how "now all the students have, you know, these very different names," Amanda summarized:

> I think the biggest thing I learned is to try to, like, get over that and just move on and, and try to, and generally be respectful for what anybody might say and not really worry about specifically where they're coming from [meaning what country or racial/ethnic group(s)] unless they bring up, like, I guess to be open to diversity but not to stress it or push it. To allow it to kind of come out as it does but not to, to seek it out [by asking students to talk about themselves in front of the class].

Despite her efforts at openness, Amanda's language (e.g., "these very different names") suggests that she was still using her own white, middle-class experience as the norm. At the same time, though to a lesser extent than before, she was feeling like an outsider. She volunteered that:

> [O]ne of the things I'm actually feeling kind of lucky about is that my cooperating teacher is African American. And I feel like I'm getting a, definitely a different perspective. . . . I think that she, she in some ways is able to connect on a different level with some of the students, being a minority, um, and she feels, I think she feels more authentic too, kind of doing some of, like the multicultural literature and all that, and, um,

you know, she reads some of, like, the slang words and, and it doesn't sound like she's sounding 'em out, you know, like she knows how to say them [both interviewer and Amanda laugh] and, you know, and maybe that's a stereotype too but, but I kinda feel lucky to be getting that perspective and to be learning from somebody who, maybe connects on that level with the students.

Although Amanda's co-op may know how to pronounce "the slang words," as a middle- to upper-middle-class professional, she likely has had to learn them, too. Amanda is oversimplifying or overstating the connection between her co-op and the African American students in her classes as well as overgeneralizing about African Americans as a group. At the same time, Amanda's fallback to her own experience and feeling like an outsider is understandable given her limited experience in an urban high school with a diverse student population.

The "multicultural literature" that Amanda refers to is that written by authors of color. In New York, this usually means African American, Hispanic, Asian, or Native American authors. (These are New York State's official designations of "underrepresented" groups.) At Royalton, the focus would be on African American and Hispanic as well as canonical white authors (e.g., Shakespeare, Poe). Amanda was just beginning to see value in including a wider range of authors than she had studied in high school as a way of connecting with her students academically. She commented that she saw "a push by some teachers to include more multicultural literature" and that the 11th-grade American literature textbook has "a wide diversity in it." In the 11th-grade class of another teacher, Amanda observed them "doing" Christmas literature, including a piece written by a black author "well known for writing about black women," Toni Cade Bambara's "Christmas Eve at Johnson's Drugs and Goods."

And the kids are really into it because for a lot of them it, it speaks to them, it has some more of their language in it, um, so I guess I've seen, like, little ways in which they embrace it there, and I think that works. But I haven't seen a huge focus on it as a divisive factor.

While Amanda clearly sees the value in "multicultural" literature for engaging African American and Hispanic students, she still struggles with concerns about divisiveness and neglecting the canonical literature that she studied in high school. Similarly, as will be shown, she struggles between understanding her students' out-of-school lives and upholding "school expectations," including attendance and homework. Looking forward to student-teaching, she quips, "as much as I want to get out there, I'm, it's [laughs], kind of like jumping off a cliff, and you really hope the parachute opens."

Cora: "Spark Their Interests"

Recall (from Chapter 2) that Cora saw her major challenges at Royalton High School as connecting with her students both personally and academically, teaching differently from her cooperating teacher (in order to engage students and foster critical thinking), and classroom management. Despite the negative external messages about urban schools that she reported, her "white girl" concerns, and her very limited prior experience with difference and diversity, Cora seemed genuinely eager to get to know her students. She hoped to learn from them as well as to teach them science.

Cora said that she liked Royalton's racial/ethnic diversity and difference from her own high school, which she described as "kind of sheltered from everything like I was just living in this little bubble." She also recognized that the influences of the poverty, gangs, and violence found in some Royalton students' neighborhoods did not simply evaporate when the students entered the school. She said, "I know it's really tough for kids to have to deal with, and it's not easy to just shrug it off when you walk into the doors of the school. So, it obviously follows them in." Very few of the prospective teachers we followed explicitly acknowledged their own "little bubble," or the family and neighborhood challenges that their students might be facing.

Cora's empathy for her students extended to the cuts in extracurricular activities because of the district's severe budget problems. She referred specifically to the music program and the hallway displays from "the old shows they used to do" and how it is "really pretty sad that they cannot do that anymore, 'cus I thought that that would be, like, a great way to, like, get the kids, like, expressing themselves and taking pride in their school and in their work and things like that." Later, she noted that Royalton High School and its students had fewer resources than some of the selective city schools and most suburban schools:

> they don't have the same amounts of technology in the classroom. . . . [T]hey don't have the after-school programs . . . they have huge class sizes, like, they have two guidance counselors for the entire school, they have two assistant principals for the entire school, like, I just don't feel like they're getting a fair shake.

She summarized: "I definitely think they get shafted."

Returning to the challenge of connecting with her students personally, Cora was uncertain about when and how much to share about herself. Although Cora said that she did not know how much to tell students about herself initially "without getting too personal," she wanted them to know that "I am not the white girl from the suburban school with the two parents . . . and the family kind of thing. That is not how I grew up. . . . I didn't have the greatest, easiest life either, and look where it gets, you can get anywhere." From a "single-parent family" that was "on welfare" for a while, Cora is offended by and rails against the common belief that children from such homes don't do as well in school or go as far. "I mean, it happens on average, probably, but for me it's just, like, well, that's not how it happened, and I don't think you should generalize people that way. . . . [P]eople can make it despite their background."

When I asked Cora what parallels, if any, she saw between her experience with peers' and others' assumptions about "single-parent homes" and similarly negative assumptions about African American kids or poor kids or city kids in general, she responded:

> I think people in both cases have very, like, set preconceived notions about who these people are and how they are going to act before they even meet them. Just because of what they have heard and maybe what they have seen on TV. . . . So, it's definitely an uphill kind of struggle I guess. For me personally, I think it is less because I didn't, I let people get to know me first before I tell them that kind of information just so they don't make prejudgments. . . . [T]hey gotta get to know me first before I am going to tell them that kind of stuff. And it is a lot harder to do, like, with race and things like that because it is right there. So, I don't know, I think it is a more difficult struggle in that respect, but I can see the parallels as far as like people's ideas.

In response to my question about the possibility that her experience might be an advantage at Royalton, Cora said, "I think I am more open-minded and can relate better to the students at [Royalton]. I know what it is like to struggle. I know what it is like to have a parent on welfare." Cora also recognized her advantage in being white and the relative "invisibility" now of her earlier poverty. Although Cora's experiences growing up seem to have fostered empathy for her students who are experiencing similar situations, she also was adamant that "you can still make it."

At the same time, Cora expressed reservations about difference and diversity, suggesting that there was some tension between her new experiences and learnings and her prior beliefs. Asked what she had learned about dealing constructively with difference at Royalton, Cora said:

> I have been able to experience all the different diversity. I mean basically constructively, I just I just treat them like everybody else. [Laugh] I don't try and say "oh, you're this race or this race, so there-

fore I am going to treat you this way or this way." So I guess I am just starting to see everybody in the same way. I mean obviously you have to pay attention to people's needs. And, like, you know, if you notice a student struggling and things like that you have to be able to, like, say "hey what's going on?"

Cora did not specify the "them" whom she treats like "everybody else," what that treatment entails, or what it means to "see everybody in the same way." It sounded like a version of so-called colorblindness that sees middle-class whiteness as the standard.

Cora also referred to university classes where they "talked about multi-cultural education and things like that . . . like ethnic pride . . . celebrating diversity," which she said she agreed with: "like I think it needs to be ad-dressed . . . our country's one that's, like, all sorts of races put together." "But," she continued, "then again you think, 'well, really we are all, like, Americans anyway,' so I don't know." When pressed, she said that she didn't know how to put the multicultural education theories into practice. Acknowledgement of other cultures was all right, she said, but celebrat-ing was not, and it was impossible to address every group. "I just think we should all just celebrate America, not just pigeonhole everybody as just one thing. Because, like, really now that we are all here, just celebrate that."

Part of Cora's concern about pigeonholing people by racial or ethnic group seems to be related to her more general opposition to group labels and stereotyping. She also mentions that people may be more than "one thing." Like Amanda, she associated diversity with divisiveness. "I just think by trying to segregate ourselves through race, it just keeps the sepa-ration going, like, I mean we're never going to be a united society if we keep dividing ourselves like that." The united or unified society Cora has in mind is one where people see "each other for people rather than 'oh, you're this or you're that.' Just, you know, getting to know how we're all the same, like, the same but different." She thought that it would be diffi-cult for people to identify with both their particular racial/ethnic culture and a more encompassing American society and culture.

It seems to me that Cora was still carrying conservative baggage from her white, small town–rural upbringing and struggling with the tensions between those beliefs and her new experiences and professional goals. Asked how her beliefs about difference and diversity had changed since the beginning of the school year, Cora said:

> Well, I'm more aware it's out there. . . . I am not more, like, turned off
> by it or anything. Actually it's, I am more interested in it now than I
> was before since I am being exposed to it, 'cus I wanna get to know

their [students'] backgrounds and who they are and stuff like that. I take a more active interest I guess.

Cora's desire to connect with her students personally and academically meant getting to know them, part of which meant "their backgrounds and who they are" beyond their identity as a person, human being, or an American.

In our second conversation at the end of Field Experience and just prior to student-teaching, Cora described continuing to get to know her students, for example, by helping out during labs and talking with students, and observing others, including a special education class. She continued to rail against lumping, labeling, and stereotyping students (e.g., as dumb or as hoodlums) and "the whole self-fulfilling prophecy thing." In this regard, it is noteworthy that Cora acknowledged learning that Royalton was more racially/ethnically diverse than she thought initially. Like Ken, Jaclyn, and a few of the other prospective teachers we followed, she had seen the school as overwhelmingly African American. Now, she said, "I've seen more whites in classes with Hispanics, blacks, you know, it's a better mix than I had originally noticed."

Another key event was what, from Cora's description, appeared to be a spontaneous class discussion following several fights at the school about why some students lash out violently. Cora related that:

> [A] couple of the students actually started to talk about, like, their own backgrounds and their own personal life, which I thought was pretty open, I mean, to say in front of the whole class . . . some of the stuff they went through [e.g., physical abuse, parent(s) in jail, foster care] is pretty awful, so, I mean, I guess on that kind of level I, like, connected with them a little bit, got to know more about them and their background.

Asked how that information might help her work with her students, Cora used homework as an example:

> [W]e as teachers are, like, "oh, you know, go home and read this chapter, go home and do this homework, it's the most important thing you need to do," where really, like, if you take that into consideration with what's really going on in the rest of their lives, school sometimes takes a backseat, and I think you have to be at least a little bit understanding of that by knowing their background.

Later, Cora told us that her cooperating teacher said that she "had no idea about hardly any of these students and what they're going through." "I was like, 'wow, that's a problem' . . . that she doesn't know her students all that well . . . obviously, you're not gonna pry into everything, but you should know them a little bit."

Cora went on to say that although she has not personally experienced the things that some of her students have gone through, just knowing about it "makes it a lot different for me in my mind when I think of, like, really how important is it [e.g., homework], you know, I mean, in the grand scheme of things. It's good that they're even in school." But, as will be shown, school expectations, such as completing homework and other assignments, do matter, and Cora, like Amanda, finds herself taking both sides. Realizing that students have things other than school going on in their lives, things that sometimes take priority for them, is one thing. Deciding how to work with that realization without giving up on academic teaching and learning is another.

In addition to learning some things about some of her students' lives outside of school, their preferred music, and the TV shows they watched, Cora mentioned learning more about informal language, how to teach students with lower reading levels, and how "you've got to change it up and, like, each student is different in, like, how they learn."

Amanda and Cora: Struggling Toward Academic Teaching and Learning

Both Amanda and Cora reached out to connect with their students academically and to foster meaningful learning. At the same time, they struggled with appropriate expectations for their students. Amanda cited "expectations" as one of the biggest problems she encountered in working with students whose backgrounds and experiences differed from hers. Once again, she referred to her own high school experience in an affluent suburb where, for example, college was a goal toward which most students worked. At Royalton, in contrast, "students expected not to do homework . . . students didn't care if they missed things, if they even read . . . it was just like a whole different attitude . . . a lot of their, just their life experiences were so different." The appropriate expectations that were a continuing struggle for Amanda also involved literature selection. She said that while she tried to vary the authors she selected for students to read, she also asked herself:

> "Am I picking this author because they are a good author, or am I picking this author because I think culturally it will relate to the students?" And, you know, especially with, like, English, you need to, you know, there are so many really good authors from all cultures, but, you know, there's like, a, kinda, like a canon that is expected to be taught.

With my freshmen it was easy because we taught *Romeo and Juliet* so, like, you know, so that is what I just taught. Um, again they, a lot of times, you know, we try to relate it to things in their lives like gangs and things like that. But that was, you know, I probably wouldn't have done it as much at a suburban school that didn't have a gang issue.

An autobiography project that Amanda introduced later in her student-teaching at Royalton revealed much more about her students' backgrounds than she had known previously and raised further questions about bridge-building and fairness. Like Cora, she was amazed at how much students shared about themselves:

We had people crying when they were presenting their autobiographical projects because they really gave their personal details . . . so many of my students have experienced tragedy, and I am not sure if this is a cultural thing or, but experienced tragedy well beyond my comprehension. . . . [L]ike even coming from, like, I came from a family where my dad had been married 4 times. You know, I have seen, like, three messy divorces and, but, like, still to me I have always had this very basic foundation of a normal family life. And, you know, to find out that these students didn't have that, sometimes it was easy to see why they have the problems they do. At the same time I had to separate that from school [expectations], well still taking it into account. Like, so, it was hard, you know, it was hard to take care of all that information. [S]ometimes it is hard to not be overly sympathetic to students that, you know, have really bad home lives or really bad backgrounds and to still hold them to the same standards, because you really wanna be, like . . . "Can you give them an extra ten points if they pass this?" You know, you can't be like that, but it's hard to not take those personal situations and worry about them.

Recall Cora's recognition of how difficult it is for some students to find time, a place, and the energy and concentration to do homework with everything that is going on in their lives. Despite that recognition, she folded turning in homework on time into classroom management (perhaps at her co-op's urging), where it was imperative to enforce the rules or risk losing control.

I tend to be sort of a laid-back kind of person, so for me to have to be, like, laying down the law on these kids, it was pretty tough, but I just started, you know. They knew that if they didn't have their homework handed in, it was a zero, there was no way around it. If you come in late to class, it's detention after school, there's no way around that.

Cora rejected what she saw as the widespread assumption that "these kids are either just gonna drop out or get minimum wage jobs, so why bother, which is pretty sad." At the same time, she recognized that some students had weak reading skills and/or difficult home lives that interfered with conventional schoolwork; it was not necessarily the case that these students or their parents just "didn't care." Cora offered her 9th-grade Living Environment class as an example of the wide range of student skill and motivation at Royalton. Because of some students' low reading level, she said, they sometimes read in class, "underlining the important concepts in the paragraphs [and she asked questions about meanings and provided examples] . . . we really had to, like, slow it down, which was fine," but this would "take away" from what they could do otherwise with the students who "get it right away." Cora said that she could not always distinguish whether the weaker students lacked motivation and/or skills: "it was hard to tell 'cause I don't know how many of these students played dumb, so they don't look smart in front of their peers. I know some people would hide their intelligence very well in front of their peers just to make sure nobody saw." Unfortunately, too often, these students "hide their intelligence" from their teachers as well, which feeds low expectations and a self-defeating cycle of minimal teaching and learning.

The struggle here is obvious, and there is no one best way to deal with, let alone resolve, the various problems that students bring to school. Extra points? More time to complete assignments? Grading based on improvement rather than a fixed standard? Personal encouragement and assistance? This is a conundrum where individualizing, treating each case in its own context, is desirable. As both Cora and Amanda observed, there is no universal motivation or way to reach all students all the time: "you're not gonna' get everybody, but you can get some" (Cora). Amanda put it this way: "I just never did figure out how to get around . . . just trying to find individual students' motivation. It was really hard to find universal things." And what "worked" might not last long (see Chapter 2).

A related concern, one not explicitly voiced by Cora or Amanda, involves the trade-offs between "cutting students a break" and upholding academic expectations. Too much sympathy for students' situations could lead to patronizing them, lower academic expectations, and less teaching-learning, which could not help students in the longer run because it limits their future opportunities. Both Cora and Amanda appeared to reject this option. Amanda commented, "I really do feel like we are doing an injustice to students by not providing them with the same education [as suburban students]. And part of it is because they're not being held to the same standards."

A more constructive alternative involves examining expectations and assignments and asking of each: "How important is it?" Perhaps, for example, the frequency of homework could be reduced with the understanding that the assignments given are important and are expected to be completed on time. Extra time might be allotted, occasionally and on an individual basis, if it is requested in advance, not when the assignment is due. Alternatively, perhaps only eight of 10 or 12 homework assignments or three of five quizzes will "count" in each grading period.

While some prospective (and experienced) teachers focus on classroom management (see Ken and Lynn in Chapter 5), Amanda rarely mentioned it, and Cora's initial concerns faded. She told us:

> Once I was there for awhile, it became a little easier, so it was fine. . . . I definitely had a handful of students that were very disruptive [e.g., making dramatic, attention-getting entrances to class] . . . but I would say that on the whole, the vast majority of these kids would sit down and do their work. I mean, it might take a little while to get settled down, but once they got on task, they were good to go.

Particularly noteworthy is Cora's comment that she felt "like, the good kids sort of get pushed to the wayside, because they're [teachers, administrators, media] so focused on getting the other kids in line, that small percentage."

With few exceptions, both Cora and Amanda kept their focus on "the good kids" and tried to draw in more students. Ways in which they attempted to reach more students included making themselves available, moving among students to "see how they're doing on an assignment" (Cora) and offering assistance as needed, trying to "make it as real as possible, like . . . bring it down a few notches and try to relate it to their lives so that it did make sense to the majority" (Cora), and using different ways of presenting ideas and information (e.g., visually as well as verbally). Cora succeeded, slowly and "in baby steps," in involving her students in activities like small-group projects—weaning them from "the notes" that were her co-op's mainstay as she gained confidence in managing a classroom. She told us that:

> I just tried as hard as I could to make it interesting for everyone. . . . I gave it my best shot trying to get them involved, trying to get them to do things, whether I was met with a heavy sigh or whatever, I would just, you know, be persistent with them, and be, like, "you know, come on, this is something that could relate to your life, you've heard of this," you know.

Cora's account of encouraging and prodding students is similar to Amanda's (see Chapter 2) and what Kate, also a prospective science teacher, described while working with a different cooperating teacher the previous year (see Chapter 2). Importantly, none of these prospective teachers could have succeeded in being "persistent" had they not already established positive relationships with their students. Cora, Kate, and Amanda acted on the belief that, in Cora's words, "teachers shouldn't just write their students off, certain students off," as if they would "never amount to anything."

As an English teacher, Amanda had more opportunity than Cora to select subject matter (e.g., plays, poems, stories) and assignments that were likely to appeal to her students' experience and interest. She could select a black author in response to student requests during Black History Month. Later, she selected a Hispanic author and was surprised by some of her Hispanic students' responses. Some who rarely if ever actively participated in class "were excited because it [the book] had Hispanic [*sic*] words." She continued:

> [T]hey became the experts, they got to pronounce the words, and they loved it. Some of my black students were like, "What is this all about? Aren't we going to read anymore black authors?" They noticed the change, and it wasn't even, uh, a conscious change on my part. As a matter of fact, the reason why I chose the book [*The House on Mango Street* by Sandra Cisneras] was because I was taught it in my Strategies class and thought it fit well with the theme of what we were doing. It really wasn't like I said, "I need to teach a Hispanic author," it was "I want to teach this book."

Both Amanda and her African American students might have experienced a bit of consciousness-raising with this novel, specifically that diversity in the United States is more than black and white. Amanda also is learning that students respond well to seeing people like themselves in the curriculum in proactive ways, not only as victims (e.g., enslaved, conquered, or interned peoples) or problems (e.g., poor, illiterate). This experience can be eye-opening for other students as well.

By the end of student-teaching at Royalton, Amanda and Cora were experiencing some success building bridges between their own and their students' worlds toward meaningful teaching and learning. Despite rough spots and detours, they persevered (as they urged students to do in their classes), and they gained satisfaction from both the effort and the students' responses. Cora, for example, described gaining a "dose of reality," but still being "enthusiastic and ready to go change the world, it's just, maybe I'm not as, like, wide-eyed as I was."

Importantly, both prospective teachers expressed strong equity concerns, specifically that Royalton students were not getting "a fair shake" (Cora) or were being set up to fail (Amanda). Cora argued that:

[T]he school should definitely be a place where kids are treated equally regardless of, you know, economic status, any of that, learning ability, any of that kind of a thing. All students should be given a fair shake at it . . . school should be the place where these kids can get away from, like, their societal constraints, like, you know, income, family, whatever. . . . [T]eachers shouldn't just write their students off, certain students off. They shouldn't say "oh, this kid will never amount to anything, so why should I even bother?" I think all teachers need to treat all their students as if, you know, they're someone who matters. Therefore, they should be getting the same education as everybody else in this classroom, whether they think these students care or not, so I think teachers need to stay dedicated to all their students, not just some of their students.

Amanda's experience at Royalton, and perhaps with the teacher education program more generally, appeared to prompt major changes in her perspective about equity and social justice:

Well, my mentality before I became a teacher was definitely, like, those kids' parents pay for it, they deserve it. And I think that's 'cus I grew up in an affluent suburb, so I felt, you know, my parents paid for it, so I got it. So, that is the way the world should work. Um [pause] but I see now, like, the lack of resources has such a huge impact and how we're, like, setting students up to fail, because we are setting them up to not be able to function in college because they are not being given homework, because there aren't books for them to take home, and it's like an endless cycle, so if they do go to college, like, they might not have developed good homework skills, and they may not have developed independent reading skill, because they are not being asked to read independently. So, I think in that way, like, we're kind of as a culture, like, as a society setting ourselves up to fail.

Recall Amanda's amazement at the lack of books for students to read or study at home and the "make-do" attitude of teachers (see Chapters 2 and 3). Now, she suggested having a regional warehouse where English teachers could go to sign out 150 copies of the book they wanted to use, such as Harper Lee's *To Kill a Mockingbird*. The experience at Royalton, she said, "made me, like, wish there was more collaboration to kind of equal the playing field." She concluded that by not holding students to mainstream standards, academically and behaviorally, "we are doing an injustice to students" because they are not going to be able to hold a job even at McDonald's. "The reality is they [students] still need to fit into our [middle-class, adult] society to be successful. . . . [U]nfortunately, they are probably going to have to learn the hard way." Although one might object to the social reality that Amanda describes, it is difficult to argue that her description is inaccurate, except perhaps for the select few celebrities of the moment.

BUILDING AND MAINTAINING BRIDGES

Kate, a prospective science (earth science) teacher, and Malcolm, a prospective social studies (global history) teacher, both in the first year of our project, appeared to feel comfortable with student difference and diversity almost immediately. They had a strong sense of purpose about how they wanted to teach and what they wanted their students to learn, and they worked hard to realize their goals. A major difference in their experience at Royalton was that Malcolm's cooperating teacher was supportive of his critical thinking and social justice goals while Kate's co-op opposed her critical thinking and active learning goals for students.

Connecting with students personally seemed to be taken for granted by both Kate and Malcolm. Kate, for example, told me, "it's amazing how easy it is to build relationships" with Royalton students. She said all you needed to do was just ask them a question. Students are "very willing to share themselves once you showed interest." She said that diversity was not a concern (she had worked in several school programs with students from a range of backgrounds), but that this was her first experience with high school students. There were student behavior problems, but nothing that Kate felt was a result of her background being different from her students'. Rather, she said, the students' difficult out-of-school environment was expressed in classroom behavior: "I don't think I had any negative relationships with any of my students. Ummm, not that they were all, like, excellent and positive, but certainly no negative, no bad, like, no kids I would butt heads with constantly or anything like that."

Kate expected to have to work continually on classroom management and student motivation or connecting with students academically, which she saw as her greatest challenges at Royalton. Recall (see Chapter 2) Kate's description of her pushing her students to do the activities that required some "figuring out." There would be good days and bad ones, but she was not permanently discouraged by the bad days. Kate described her seventh-period class as "just my most difficult. I would have days where they would drive me absolutely crazy, but then I would have other days where they were just so good for me and, like, so much fun to be around." Kate noted that, unfortunately, behavior problems and apathy meant that you did not accomplish as much as you would in a school situation where just about all the students are cooperative and participating. She said, "These kids aren't getting the same education."

Malcolm had worked with African Americans and other people of color as well as limited-English-speaking whites, so he was not concerned about difference and diversity *per se*. He did admit to being "a bit apprehensive to walk in" to Royalton because of prior misconceptions and stereotypes from reading, media accounts, and other people's comments about urban schools. "I tried not to have any expectations," he said, "but everyone has expectations when you go into a school." Malcolm found, however, that Royalton "wasn't anything like I thought it was gonna be." He continued:

> I thought the kids were gonna be bigger. Um, they were small. They were, they were children, you know? It was happy, um, the school was clean, um, it was well-lit, everything was, uh, nice. The students were extremely friendly. Uh, I didn't see a lot of the [sighs], I don't know, the violent aspects that I guess you read about and stuff that you hear about how bad things can be. I saw a lot of positives, actually. Um, you know, I saw students talking and having a good time and, for the most part, being somewhat attentive. I mean, there are obviously problems in classrooms with, you know, paying attention and stuff like that but overall, I was just, like, "Wow, this is gonna be a great experience."

Malcolm saw student engagement as his greatest challenge (see Chapter 2) and continually worked hard on drawing students in, guiding them toward comprehension and figuring things out. That meant, as he learned, taking small steps, putting global history in terms that students could understand, providing encouragement, and being persistent. While ignoring negative advice from other teachers (see Chapter 3), Malcolm sought assistance from a special education teacher as well as his co-op in designing activities to reach students with varying interests and abilities. Although he said that he was not as successful as he had hoped to be with critical thinking, questioning, and social issues, Malcolm did not give up. After completing his student-teaching at Royalton, Malcolm told me, "that's still my number one goal. . . . I think that just lends itself to better learning and . . . a good classroom. . . . I think I saw a little bit of a turnaround with students at [Royalton], but it wasn't . . . what I hoped it would be."

Malcolm noted, as had Amanda and other prospective teachers at Royalton, that "there's just so many other, just, things, big things going on in their lives and within the school that . . . I think it's hard for some of those students to really focus their attention . . . where you might have seen it one day, but then it's just gone the next." So, you just keep at it and try to get students to "step outside their comfort zone and try this something new" instead of copying definitions or "notes" from the chalkboard.

Like several of the other prospective teachers we followed, Malcolm interpreted our questions about diversity in terms of racialized divisiveness or problems, which he had not encountered at Royalton. He said:

> I guess when I hear the word *diversity*, it's just, you know, black students, white students. I really don't think of it in those terms. I just think, I don't know, they're just kids. I don't worry about that necessarily. I don't worry about that, um, primarily most of my students are black and, or Latino, and they all kinda have the same kinda cultural attitude. Um, I'm more focused on, like, the way that the students are learning or who they are in terms of, like, how they participate . . . the work they do in class, stuff like that. . . . [M]y classes they seem to, like, get along. . . . I don't see any of the, kinda like, something that's gonna turn into a fight.

Initially, Malcolm said that his co-op was uneasy about his trying group work and similar activities, "but as time went on, and I built rapport with these kids," he relaxed. In contrast, Kate's experience with her co-op was much more difficult and probably would have worn down most prospective teachers as it did Renee (see Chapter 3).

As previously described (see Chapters 2 and 3), Kate's co-op objected to her efforts to do projects or give students "questions that asked them to not just take from the book and write it on the worksheet, but to think about what they did in the lab or think about what it talks about in the book and expand upon that, you know, a higher level of thinking basically." She told me:

> It was a real battle for a while. . . . [H]e just couldn't understand why I wanted them to do this activity, or why I wanted to do it this way, and he would be, like, "why don't you just give them notes?" or, you know, "Why don't you just run off copies?" . . . I would explain why I wanted to do it this way, and he'd be, like . . . "I am the experienced teacher, and I know how to do it right, and I'll tell you in this not so direct way that your way is wrong."

He believed that "your job is to show them how it works, you know, it's not to let them figure it out," and he advised Kate not to expect too much from the students or to push them too hard. Further, Kate said, "he has openly admitted to me that he teaches how he learned best, but he doesn't see anything wrong with that" for these students at this time and place. She realized later that her co-op also cared about her and did not want to see her fail because of classroom management problems. She was his first student-teacher.

Kate persisted, sought assistance from other teachers when she wanted to try something new, and eventually wore down her co-op. According to Kate:

> I think after a while, and it kind of almost took badgering from some of the other teachers to be, like, "leave her alone," that he finally loosened up. It was, like, the last couple weeks . . . he was, like, "no, do, do whatever" and finally got off my back a little bit, and I could do a little more.

By getting to know their students and using the positive relationships to prod and support students academically, Kate and Malcolm gained their students' respect (most of their students, most of the time) and achieved small successes. Their strong sense of purpose and the time, energy, and thoughtfulness that they put into their work as student-teachers paid off in student learning and their own sense of accomplishment. They paid a price, too, for example, in separating themselves from negative colleagues (and often eating lunch alone) and Kate's risking her co-op's negative evaluation.

As the experiences of teachers elsewhere show, high teacher expectations and persistence can have negative effects if there is no mutual respect between teacher and students. Hemmings (2003) describes Ms. Thomas, a new AP (Advanced Placement) English teacher at Central City High "who was determined to implement more intellectually rigorous practices [and] . . . worked very hard to position herself as an authority figure who not only had the right to direct all classroom activities but also deserved the utmost respect from students" (p. 423). It did not work. The more she persevered in demanding respect and obedience, the more the students resisted.

In contrast, Ms. Hathaway, a math teacher at the same school, "was described by just about every senior as the most respected teacher in the school" (Hemmings, 2003, p. 432). At least two factors seem to explain her success: the respect she demonstrated for her students and her instructional approach in showing students how to do something, not simply telling them to "do it." Hemmings provides this account:

> "She makes everyone sit up straight when she walks in the room," Michael said. "Like, no one gives her any crap." What set Ms. Hathaway off from Ms. Thomas was how she made learning strategies explicit and practically manageable for students. She would march her classes through lessons in a

step-by-step, this-is-how-you-do-it fashion and provide whatever direct assistance students needed to complete assigned tasks. Something else that set Ms. Hathaway off was the high level of civility in her relations with students. Students were never rude to her nor did they use profanity, make jokes, or otherwise sabotage lessons with disrespectful remarks. The respect shown to this teacher was expressed in recognition of her instructional competence and appreciation for the respect she had for inner-city Black kids as students who can and will learn if they are shown exactly how. (p. 432)

Students who have been shortchanged educationally, for whatever reasons, need and deserve enriched teaching, not the "dumbed-down," rote drill and practice that too often is what they get nor demanding assignments with little or no instruction that might enable students to complete them satisfactorily.

Rich examples of other newer and more experienced black, white, and Hispanic teachers who successfully bridge the different worlds of schooling and students are offered by Ladson-Billings (1994), Michie (2005), and Sleeter (2005).

CONCLUSIONS

During the time I was writing this chapter (the summer of 2007), a major interstate highway bridge over the Mississippi River in Minnesota collapsed during evening rush hour, resulting in at least a dozen deaths and many more injuries as well as extensive physical destruction. In addition to feelings of distress and uneasiness shared by many, I wondered about my use of the bridging metaphor here. It fits, I concluded. Even the best-built bridges do not last forever, and certainly not very long without appropriate maintenance and repair. There are different kinds of bridges, for different situations. As conditions change, bridges may need to be rebuilt or replaced. Just as there is no one best bridge, there is no one best practice for bridging different worlds in school. The successful but imperfect bridging by prospective and experienced teachers illustrated here can provide grounds for hope and wise practice by other new teachers elsewhere.

7

Where Do We Go from Here?

In this concluding chapter, I do more than sum up or lament that more research or money for teacher education is needed. A summary will not move us forward, and not just any research or use of additional resources will benefit prospective and newer teachers or their students in urban schools like Royalton or Charter School. The patterns of new teacher engagement with student difference and diversity portrayed in previous chapters, together with the relevant scholarly literature such as that about culturally relevant or responsive teaching, have clear implications for teacher education and teaching. Considering those implications, including what would be involved in acting on them, is my purpose here. In so doing, I try to speak directly to both prospective and newer teachers and to teacher educators, and indirectly to administrators and policymakers. If we wait for most administrators and policymakers to do more than tinker around the edges of teacher education, precious little will happen that is of benefit to poor students, students of color, or students whose first language is not English. As a result, all of us will suffer in one way or another. I welcome your responses (ccorn@buffalo.edu).

Several of these implications for preservice and inservice teacher education policy and practice run counter to, or cut across the grain of, conventional wisdom and/or recent and ongoing "reform" movements. This is because, I have come to believe, more than modest changes within the system and institutions of teacher education are needed. Most calls for reform call for changes *within* the system, not changes *to* the system itself. This pretty much business-as-usual approach may make those involved feel good, but the positive effects do not usually extend to most students in urban schools. Ironically, "tinkering" changes such as adding a multicultural course or a field experience in an urban school is like adding special features to school textbooks in order to make them appear more diverse or multicultural. The "blue pages" or boxed features are set apart from the text or main story, which does not change. They are add-ons or decorations that are buried by the main story, just as the multicultural course is overwhelmed by the rest of the teacher education program that remains unchanged. Unfortunately, the faculty who ridicule the superficial changes in textbooks often seem not to see the parallels in their own teacher education programs. (Similar arguments could be made about school reform, but school system reform is beyond the scope of this volume.)

Others have written eloquently about needed changes in teacher education to better serve our changing school population (e.g., Ladson-Billings, 1999a; Villegas & Lucas, 2002; Nieto, 2003) with too little evidence of impact to date. I suspect that this is because more than superficial changes are needed, such changes have been called for only recently, and they run counter to the prevailing assumptions of standardization. It will take many voices, from different directions, before the message will be widely heard, let alone acted upon. Here, the intent is to add my rather brusque voice to the call for more coherent and context-sensitive teacher preparation.

IMPLICATIONS FOR TEACHER EDUCATION AND TEACHING

The implications that are clear to me and that I share in the following sections go from the simpler and easier to put into practice to the more complex and difficult:

1. Getting along or surviving in an urban school should not be mistaken for teaching students.
2. A "good" teacher is not good for all students, and is not as good for some students as for others.
3. Currently, teacher education programs offer too much on difference and diversity in general, and too little that is specific enough to be helpful.
4. Greater emphasis and resources should be placed at the school sites in order to work more intensively with prospective teachers in the field.
5. Tackle (1) understanding one's own identities and positioning, (2) colorblindness and white privilege, (3) de-centering oneself and one's expectations/cultural assumptions, and (4) cultural and institutional racism.
6. Use program admissions criteria, especially in areas where supply exceeds demand, to discourage prospective teachers who are not open to difference and diversity.
7. Retire the old teacher education debates, and consider contemporary questions.

Surviving Versus Teaching

Especially for new teachers who have little knowledge about and experience with diverse groups of people who are different from themselves or are fearful of urban schools and students, it is much too easy to mistake getting along for teaching. There is a sense of relief that comes with getting to know your students, even if you do not know them very well. Finding that they are not "that bad," you get along. At this point, however, some prospective teachers are satisfied with going through the motions of teaching, such as presenting information, assigning and collecting worksheets, and giving tests. They do not push themselves or their students into meaningful teaching and learning—meaningful in the sense that they go beyond rote memorization of presumably factual information to comprehension and critical thinking that incorporates diverse perspectives. They tend to believe that their students cannot do more challenging work, that more active student involvement in open-ended activities will result in their loss of classroom control, or that students will reject thinking for themselves and figuring things out in favor of getting or copying right answers. Both teachers and students are content to get along, get through the day, and survive. Unfortunately, both Ken and Lynn illustrate this form of survival, as do veteran teachers who are described as "burnt out."

A variation on this evasion of teaching is more seductive. Students in schools like Royalton usually respond favorably to their teachers showing a personal interest in them, perhaps because positive attention from adults is scarce in their lives, or because they see a way of conning prospective and newer teachers out of asking them to do much work, or simply because it's enjoyable. In any event, the teachers, in turn, feel appreciated and needed. Two graduate students who recently completed the same teacher education program but were not part of our project offered unsolicited comments about how, compared to suburban students, urban students at Royalton and a nearby high school really made you feel needed and appreciated (i.e., good) if you just showed a little bit of interest in them. Feeling good about their students' response to their overtures, prospective teachers may sacrifice academics for fear of upsetting what they see as good teacher-student relationships. Instead, they should be using the good relationships to foster meaningful teaching and learning, as did Karen and several other PTs at Royalton.

Effective teachers of African American and other urban students not only hold high expectations for their students, but also assist them in meeting those expectations. Assistance takes the form of encouragement, support, and explicit instruction about how to do the assigned task. Recall Kate, for example, refusing to give in and insisting that her students could do it—and they did (encouragement), Malcolm moving his students along in small steps (support), and Ms. Hathaway, the respected inner-city math teacher who taught her students how to succeed (explicit instruction). Gloria Ladson-Billings (1994) puts it this way, based on her study of successful elementary teachers, both black and white, of African American students in a low socioeconomic status community:

1. *When students are treated as competent they are likely to demonstrate competence....* These teachers provide intellectual challenges by teaching to the highest standards and not to the lowest common denominator....
2. *When teachers provide instructional "scaffolding," students can move from what they know to what they need to know....* Rather than chastise them for what they do not know, these teachers find ways to use the knowledge and skills the students bring to the classroom as a foundation for learning.
3. *The focus of the classroom must be instructional....* The message that the classroom is a place where teachers and students engage in serious work is communicated clearly to everyone....
4. *Real education is about extending students' thinking and abilities....* Rather than a "drill-and-kill" approach to knowledge acquisition, their approach makes student learning a more contextualized, meaningful experience.
5. *Effective teaching involves in-depth knowledge of both the students and the subject matter....* [The successful teachers] know their students well. They know which ones respond to subtle prodding and which ones need a more forceful approach. For them, good teaching starts with building good relationships. (pp. 123–125, emphasis in original)

A key here is that good teaching starts, but does not end, with positive teacher-student relationships. From an oral history project based on interviews with black teachers and administrators, Michele Foster (2001) offers a similar message for teachers of African American and other students: Expect more of your students and then teach them what you want them to know.

Prospective and newer teachers should ask themselves to what extent they are taking teaching and their students seriously or merely getting along and surviving. Teacher educators, both cooperating teachers and university supervisor-mentors, should be raising the same questions with PTs, both encouraging and supporting them, and, if need be, directly teaching them, to move toward more meaningful teaching and learning.

One Size Fits All—Badly

The so-called unisex T-shirt is cut for people with long arms and no hips. Similarly, one-size-fits-all clothing fits very few people very well. It should not be surprising that a good teacher is not good for all students, or is not as good for some as for others. The presumably universal "good teacher" is a myth born of wishful thinking, thoughtlessness about its differential effects on students, and/or the abuse of standardization in the pursuit of higher test scores. There is no one best way of teaching or being a teacher in the 21st-century United States.

Instead, teachers need to be open-minded, flexible, and adaptable as they seek ways to work with their students to reach academic and related goals. They should not expect that trying to be like the teachers they admired in elementary or high school will make them successful with their heterogeneous groups of students in today's urban schools. Similarly, teacher educators in various methods classes ought not to present single methods or versions of methods (e.g., inquiry, constructivist, critical thinking) as being appropriate for all students and settings. Instead, we should demonstrate how various methods can be modified or adapted for different contexts *without watering down* the eventual outcomes—and then ask prospective and newer teachers to do the same for specific classes or groups of students.

PTs should not be able to say, legitimately, that what they learned in methods class "won't work here." If their teacher education instructors do not show them how to adapt "lessons," PTs should ask them to do so. Or, PTs can try to figure it out for themselves, just as they might ask students to do with a math problem, a science lab, a political cartoon, or an unfinished story. Amanda in English and Malcolm in social studies well illustrate appropriate adaptations. Recall Malcolm, for example, describing going slowly and taking small steps while insisting that students work out meanings for themselves rather than looking to him for answers.

Instead of asking students to make most or all of the changes or do most or all of the work, consider what classroom and teaching changes would enable more students to extend and demonstrate their academic knowledge and skills. This is an ongoing challenge for both teachers and students, not a problem that can be solved once and for all. Rather than add-ons or a "bag of tricks," think of tailoring teaching to better fit our students and build on their strengths, teaching as custom-made or "designer" rather than mass-produced or "off the rack."

Fewer Generalities, More Specifics

This implication for teaching and teacher education is related to the one-size fallacy. Several of the prospective teachers in our project referred to what they had heard called "diversity fatigue," meaning that there was too much emphasis on diversity in the teacher education program—too many readings, too much talk. The complaints came both from some PTs who acknowledged not knowing much about "others" and from PTs who fared both well and poorly in urban schools. When pressed, they said that the information they received about diversity in general or about specific groups such as African or Asian Americans was not very helpful. Also, the characterization of groups could encourage stereotyping since, for instance, not all African Americans are alike. A Ruby Payne reading about people in poverty was an example that some PTs thought was both informative and simplistic. Cora, whose family had been "on welfare" for a while, was particularly critical of Payne's portrayal. What PTs wanted, they told us, were more specifics about teaching their subject with diverse groups of students. Their students were largely black, Hispanic, and white, but also included Somalian and Sudanese refugees (both Muslim and Christian) and Russian and Chinese immigrants.

The PTs' complaints mirror the teacher education research that shows the possibility of increasing stereotypes with "textbook" descriptions of one or another group (e.g., Sleeter, 2001) as well as the promise of culturally relevant or responsive teaching that bridges the worlds of teacher and students (see Chapter 6). Culturally responsive teaching (CRT) appears to work in at least two interrelated ways. One is that students tend to respond more positively to the familiar (or seeing themselves or people like them in the curriculum) and learn more or more easily. The second is that teachers' sense of efficacy in working with students who are different from themselves is enhanced by success. Both students and teachers gain confidence and are more motivated to continue teaching and learning well. With continuing effort by all, the self-fulfilling prophecy spirals upward instead of down.

The challenge to teachers and teacher educators is that CRT cannot be prepackaged or mass-produced; it must be created anew in each classroom, in response to one's students. The task is to *learn how to learn about one's students and their cultural experiences* so as to craft culturally responsive teaching and meaningful learning opportunities. Here, I offer a sketch of the territory, with the cited references providing a fuller account. My sense of CRT follows Geneva Gay's (2000) conception:

> using the cultural knowledge, prior experiences, frames of reference, and performance styles of ethnically [and otherwise] diverse students to make learning encounters more relevant to and effective for them. It teaches *to and through* the strengths of these students. It is culturally *validating and affirming*. (p. 29, emphasis in original)

More specifically, CRT "acknowledges the legitimacy of the cultural heritages of different ethnic [and other] groups, both as legacies that affect students' dispositions, attitudes, and approaches to learning and as worthy content to be taught" (Gay, 2000, p. 29). Perhaps most importantly here, CRT "builds bridges of meaningfulness between home and school experiences as well as between academic abstractions and lived sociocultural realities" (p. 29), and does so using varied resources and multiple perspectives in order to make academic success accessible to all students.

The compatibility of these guidelines with those offered by Ladson-Billings (1994), based on her study of successful teachers of African American students, which was introduced in the previous section, adds to their credibility and raises questions about why there is so little evidence of their incorporation into teacher education programs in the United States. U.S. schools and teacher education programs in the 20th century were culturally responsive to most middle-class white students. Why, in the 21st century, do educators and teacher educators seem reluctant or unwilling to extend cultural responsiveness to most, if not all, students? No teaching or teacher education is culturally neutral.

All of us involved in teacher education ought to recognize that how *we* as well as our students "perceive the world, interact with one another, and approach learning, among other things, are deeply influenced by such factors as race/ethnicity, social class, and language" (Villegas & Lucas, 2002, p. xiv). Such understanding prepares educators "to cross the cultural boundaries that separate them from their students" (p. xiv; also see Cochran-Smith, 1995).

While some of the needed culturally relevant knowledge can be gained by prospective teachers prior to field experiences and student-teaching—in general—more specific and helpful knowledge can only be gained once you are on-site, in the school and students' homes and communities. Then you can investigate your students' "cultural knowledge, prior experiences, frames of reference, and performance styles" that are relevant to what you would like to teach them, learn how their cultural heritages might "affect their dispositions, attitudes, and approaches to learning," as well as how students' cultural heritages might be incorporated into curriculum practice. With an understanding of students' home and community experiences, their "lived sociocultural realities," one can begin to build bridges to academic learning.

Irvine (2003) emphasizes how culturally responsive teachers contextualize their teaching. To do so, they "spend more classroom and non-classroom time developing a personal relationship with their students" (p. 67), in part by listening to students' personal stories and by sharing stories about their own lives. This time investment pays dividends both in terms of student cooperation and in the teachers' ability to adapt the curriculum and instruction to be more meaningful and effective with specific students and student groups. These culturally responsive teachers:

understand and appreciate students' personal cultural knowledge and use
their students' prior knowledge and culture in teaching by constructing and
designing relevant cultural metaphors and images in an effort to bridge the
gap between what the students know and appreciate and new knowledge
or concepts to be mastered. (p. 68)

Villegas and Lucas (2002, Chapter 3) indicate topics and questions
about what teachers "need to know" about their students. Such investiga-
tion, learning, and understanding are ongoing processes. Start somewhere
and keep going. Recall Amanda's experience with incorporating black and
Hispanic authors with her students at Royalton and Fred's experience with
his transitional English class at Middle Academy. One becomes a cultural
mediator or broker as well as a teacher of English, science, or 5th-grade
math. Mediators or brokers, for example, challenge student misconceptions
or explain new concepts with cases and examples from students' everyday lives.

The culturally responsive teacher draws out and works from students'
prior knowledge and experiences. S/he incorporates cultural artifacts as
appropriate, such as family photos or traditions. S/he asks students to
compose "Where I'm From" prose poems, as illustrated by Linda Christensen and her students (2001, pp. 6–10). I have asked my graduate students
in our social studies masters program to write such poems and share them
with other students in the class, as well as with me. We then talk about
what we have learned about ourselves and one another as well as possible
uses of such an activity with students at various grade levels. Their poems
have been impressive in their variety and what students have revealed
about themselves in this context. Here are excerpts from "Where I'm From"
poems written by three students in our fall 2007 class:

I am from Ludhiana,
where the celebration of Diwali is heard for miles
in the month of November.
I am from eating smoked corn and dhal
in the bustling marketplace smelling of earthy spices.
I am from my Nana Papa's yarn shop,
where my youngest manu would pull childish antics
just so that I would be entertained.

I am from Edmonton,
where grandma and grandpa first met.
I am from the brick driveway wall,
eating popcorn, watching the fireworks on the 4th of July.

I am from Buffalo,
the faded Queen City.
I am from pouring faith and hope into sports teams
that always seem to fall just short of the coveted trophy.
I am from Buffalo, where a stiff drink and a game of darts
is always waiting.

Anjuli Dussault

I am from the family where college was mandatory although my parents never went, where things were never given but always earned, where respect and honor were our virtues, and where football pools seem to always take our money.

I am from the town that was built around an airport, where pink flamingos are not just birds but lawn ornaments, where you can still polka and celebrate Dyngus Day, where Indian names flow easily and bowling is our pastime.

I am from the region that is best known for Chicken Wings and Beef on Weck although a President was killed here, where WE, yes WE went to four consecutive Super Bowls, where it is pop not soda, Pepsi not Coke, where domestic beer includes LaBatt and Molson, and two feet of snow is not too bad. . . .

Jeff Krause

I'm a third world citizen living a super powerful dream.

This super powerful dream has opened the doors for me, but some people are afraid that these doors will bring more dreamers like me.

They have forgotten that their ancestors were dreamers just like me.

My name is Darwin Javier Rosales Maradiaga, and my name confuses people. The people in my superpower dream tell me that I don't look like a Darwin. People from my ancestry, culture, and language say that I don't look like a Darwin. . . .

Darwin Rosales

Clearly, culturally relevant knowledge goes beyond learning students' likes and dislikes or preferred music, fashion, and television programs. When prospective teachers ask about students' likes and dislikes, they often are looking for similarities in order to decrease distance and perhaps their own fear. Culturally responsive teaching pushes us further, to learn about and work with differences.

Unless teachers can respect racial/ethnic/cultural and other differences, believe that all students are able to learn, and believe that they can teach students who are different from themselves, they cannot be culturally responsive or effective. Culturally responsive teachers do not stereotype students, use only one method of teaching, use the same materials with all students, or focus on students' weaknesses. Instead, they identify and work from students' strengths in order to invite students into learning, build students' confidence, and increase success. They enrich rather than dilute curriculum and instruction.

Rich illustrations of culturally responsive teachers and teaching are provided in the sources cited here. Especially helpful resources for new teachers include Ladson-Billings (1994) and Sleeter (2005). Sleeter takes readers into the thinking and classrooms of elementary and secondary teachers who are reaching out to their primarily Mexican and Mexican American students and drawing them into academic learning, while Ladson-Billings introduces readers to the successful teachers and teaching of low-income African American elementary-age students.

Focus on What Occurs at the Schools

Given the previously cited evidence of the limited carryover from individual college/university courses to school practice and the strong influence of field experiences and student-teaching on prospective teachers, it is clear that more attention and resources should be directed to urban school sites in order to work more intensively with PTs in the field. Efforts should be directed toward guiding PTs to make sense of and act more constructively within their particular situations. If additional resources (e.g., more and better prepared personnel) are not available, then current resources can be redistributed from campus to field sites.

I can almost hear the cries of protest from faculty defending "my course," from college administrators intent on increasing student enrollments and credit-hour generation at minimal cost, from education policymakers who prefer the easy route of adding another course requirement in the name of increasing teacher quality, from university supervisor-mentors and cooperating teachers who resist change as a personal affront, and from those who believe that things are fine the way they are now. Such protests are understandable, but unconscionably self-serving and short-sighted.

After describing what is needed in the field to enable more prospective teachers to constructively and successfully engage student difference and diversity, I turn to teacher educators and program administrators to make the choices about whether and how to go about it in their particular circumstances. For example, some programs establish and maintain liaison schools and continuing relationships with staff who serve as cooperating teachers. They sponsor regular seminars where issues are raised and jointly resolved, providing staff development for both school and college personnel. These seminars could focus on how to pursue and support culturally responsive teaching, among other concerns. Other programs do not have a network of liaison schools, but they do hold seminars for a cohort of prospective teachers at each school site. Cooperating teachers could be invited to participate in some of these seminars, to address aspects of culturally responsive teaching. The challenge is not simply to decide between college/university *or* school site emphasis, but to work together for the benefit of urban teachers and their students. Student-teaching is a learning experience, not merely a limited opportunity to practice what one has learned previously.

In reviewing teacher education research relevant to *Diversity and the New Teacher*, I have been struck by evidence that field experiences and student-teaching at school sites with diverse student populations can serve to reinforce middle-class white PTs' biases or stereotypes about students who are different from themselves. This undesirable effect is more likely to occur if PTs have initial difficulty getting along and little or no support in working through their experiences, understanding what is happening both to themselves and their students, and changing course. In contrast, regular access to and/or meetings with faculty or university supervisor-mentors, who help PTs process their experiences and perhaps reframe and contextualize them, showed positive outcomes (see Sleeter, 2001). Similar findings come from a study of tutoring experiences across racial/ethnic/cultural and social class divides (Marx, 2006). Too few faculty members, university supervisor-mentors, and cooperating teachers seem to have the ability and/or the time and willingness to provide this kind of guidance. That some do, however, indicates that it can be done.

How and how well are cooperating teachers and university supervisor-mentors working together in this regard? How many student-teacher evaluation forms include items regarding constructive engagement of student difference and diversity? How do teacher education programs select and prepare their cooperating teachers and student-teacher supervisor-mentors for helping prospective teachers constructively engage diversity? In what ways do standards for teacher education policy and program accreditation address these issues?

The call here is for situation-specific guidance or assistance to prospective and newer teachers at their school sites. It can be seen as a form of CRT of teachers: getting to know new teachers and finding out where they are in relation to where the school or program would like them to be, and then working together to bridge the gap.

A last note in this section is for prospective and newer teachers who are not receiving the guidance they need or would like in constructively engaging students different from themselves: Ask! Try to be clear about the problem(s) you want help with and ask for assistance from your cooperating or mentor teacher, a respected senior teacher at the school, your university supervisor-mentor or team/department/school leader, peers, or a faculty member at your college/university.

Tackle Difficult Issues

Three related issues that are especially relevant to *Diversity and the New Teacher* but rarely addressed in U.S. teacher education programs have been touched on in previous chapters: (1) understanding one's own identities and positioning (e.g., as white, upper-middle-class, academically successful) and then de-centering oneself and one's expectations or cultural assumptions inside urban schools and classrooms; (2) the advantages and destructiveness of colorblindness and white privilege; and (3) continuing or interrupting cultural and institutional racism. As long as these issues continue to be resisted or neglected, little progress will be made toward culturally responsive teaching and constructively engaging student difference and diversity in schools and classrooms. If teacher education programs do not deal with these issues or questions, prospective and newer teachers can seek out courses, mentors, or readings that do.

I am not advocating adding another course to existing teacher education programs in order to address these issues for various political and practical as well as principled reasons, to be considered in the concluding section. Moreover, the issues appear to be best addressed on a situational, individual, or as-needed basis by supervisor-mentors, cooperating teachers, or others (see, e.g., Marx, 2006, Chapter 4) as well as within existing courses (e.g., cultural and institutional racism in social foundations of education) and/or in master's and professional development programs for already certified and practicing teachers.

For starters, see Tatum (1997, 2007) on identity development, positioning, and de-centering. The two science prospective teachers who did not constructively engage student diversity at Royalton High School, Ken and Lynn (see Chapter 5), might have benefited (as would their students) from a deeper understanding of their white, upper-middle-class, academic identities and privileged positions. This understanding might have helped them to see themselves, for example, as "fortunate" and privileged more than "normal" and then to de-center themselves and their cultural assumptions and expectations vis-à-vis their students. That would mean placing their students center-stage rather than themselves and trying to "see" their classroom and teaching from students' perspectives. Then they could focus on academic goals and getting there with their students.

Instead, we find Lynn repeatedly falling back on her background (see Chapters 2 and 5): "I am from a background where . . ." Her background or family and community culture becomes the standard from which she judges her students' cultures to be deficient. It is not the student who is the problem, she insists, but his or her culture. Ken's response is similar, although somewhat narrower, with the expectation that students should sit quietly in class, pay attention, and take notes, as he apparently did when he was in high school. He becomes exasperated by students "mostly just interrupting the class and talking to each other . . . just the talking, more than anything." "Even" the white students are unlike him. Ken comes to see the white students, as well as the African American and Hispanic students, as "definitely on a different level than me," referring specifically to their nonstandard English and troublesome attitude. Most teacher education programs are not equipped (and perhaps should not be expected) to provide as much support and redirection as PTs such as Lynn and Ken would appear to require in order to become successful teachers, especially in urban schools. Perhaps, as will be suggested in the next section, they should be "counseled out" of the program or should not be admitted in the first place.

Bell (2002) well illustrates the pitfalls of colorblindness, which she calls an "insincere fiction." You cannot engage in culturally relevant teaching if you insist on being color- or cultureblind! On white privilege, see, for instance, McIntosh (1992) for numerous examples, McIntyre (1997) on her experience examining "whiteness" with white middle- and upper-middle-class student-teachers, and Marx (2006) on her experience with white middle- and upper-middle-class prospective teachers who were tutoring students of color from working-class and poor homes.

While Kirk, who worked with 5th graders at Charter School, shares some identity development and positioning/de-centering challenges with Ken and Lynn, he more clearly represents the limits of colorblindness and associated blindness to his own white privilege (see Chapter 4). Recall that initially he described walking into Charter School as "like, complete shell shock." He was unfamiliar with and intimidated by "the ethnic diversity and stuff like that [e.g., poverty, perceived lack of parental support]" and by whites being "almost, like, outnumbered." Kirk's means of coping with his fears and negative stereotypes, especially about African Americans, was to adopt a radical individualist and colorblind perspective that takes middle-class white expectations as the norm. One should not have to deal with racial/ethnic/cultural or other difference and diversity among students;

"just treat it as a normal classroom," he told us, as if anything other than cognitive diversity were not "normal." Kirk moved from exaggerating race (e.g., the proportion of African American students at Charter School) to claiming not to see race very much, if at all. He tried to erase race and treat all students "the same."

Kirk and several other prospective and newer teachers described in previous chapters (see Chapters 4 and 5 in particular) are not only profess-ing colorblindness but also seem to be blind to their own white privilege. Colorblindness (25% of PTs in our project) was more common among ele-mentary PTs (three of four, the fourth being African American) than among secondary PTs (one of 12), perhaps because of the different school settings and/or because secondary students tend to be bigger, more assertive, and more difficult not to "see." Blindness to white privilege was widespread. If colleges and universities continue to accept students like these into their teacher education programs, they bear the responsibility of working to correct PTs' "visual impairments."

> White teachers . . . need to identify and examine their own socialization, the unearned advantages of white racial dominance, and their conscious and tacit assumptions about race and racism. All teachers need strategies for detect-ing bias in classroom and school practices, developing multicultural compe-tencies, critically analyzing and confronting racism in curriculum and school practices, and working for social justice. (Bell, 2002, p. 236)

Bell (2002) rephrases Feagin, Vera, and Batur (2001), who refer to color-blindness and its associated attitudes as "sincere fictions," in calling pro-fessed colorblindness an "insincere fiction." Avoiding these issues for fear of sounding racist or violating presumed mainstream norms of "politeness" is just as insincere and evasive. Mainstream norms serve primarily to main-tain the mainstream. Remember when "nice people" lowered their voices when they talked about divorce or cancer, or avoided mentioning such topics at all? It is past time for whispering or avoiding talk about race, ethnicity, and culture. We (white people and all teacher educators) have a lot to learn from frank talk about color, class, and culture involving diverse voices and perspectives. Bell (2002) puts it this way:

> Unless Whites can expose and examine their feelings and beliefs openly, they will continue to feel confused, will not understand the internalized racist beliefs and assumptions they keep pushing under, and will be unlikely to work effectively with students of color. (p. 240)

One way to begin the kinds of conversations and reflection advocated here is with a discussion of the thinking and actions of the prospective and newer teachers presented in Chapters 4–6 and in references cited above (Bell, 2002; Marx, 2006; McIntyre, 1997). Following analysis of others' behavior, we may be able to more honestly examine our own.

On cultural and institutional racism, see, for example, King (1991) on "dysconscious racism," Ladson-Billings (1999a) from a critical race theory perspective, and Cochran-Smith (1995) on confronting racism in teacher education. On cultural and institutional racism in U.S. society at large, see, for example, Wellman's *Portraits of White Racism* (1993); Feagin, Vera, and Batur's *White Racism* (2001); and Bonilla-Silva's *Racism Without Racists* (2006).

Cultural and institutional racism should be addressed in the U.S. history and social science coursework that PTs take as undergraduates as well as in graduate studies. Then teacher education programs can focus on how racism plays out in schooling, especially in curriculum and teaching. While social foundations of education courses play a major role here, methods and other courses also bear responsibility, e.g., for not perpetuating Eurocentric curricula or white middle-class developmental models. For example, the ubiquitous lesson plan should regularly incorporate more than one voice, perspective, or example, and should provide for more than one array of prior knowledge.

Reshape Program Admissions and Continuation

Criteria for admission to and continuation in teacher education programs should reflect what we know about more successful teaching of diverse student groups in urban and other schools. Especially in areas where supply exceeds demand, but preferably in all areas and grade levels, use program admission and continuation criteria to reject, discourage, counsel out, or eject students who lack self-confidence or comfort with themselves, desire to succeed (not merely to survive), or who are not at least moderately knowledgeable and open to racial/ethnic/cultural and other difference and diversity. More positively, program admission and continuation criteria can be used to encourage and demand self-confidence, desire to succeed, and knowledge and openness to student difference and diversity.

This probably is not welcome advice for at least two kinds of reasons. One is that it could mean fewer students and less credit-hour generation. Too many schools/colleges of education and colleges/universities count on teacher education programs as so-called cash cows to balance budgets or provide income to be spent elsewhere. They would resist such reshaping of program admission-continuation criteria—at the same time that they talk about closing achievement gaps or improving urban schooling.

A second reason is the romantically self-serving image many teacher educators have of themselves as being able to transform even the weakest or most recalcitrant PTs into "good" teachers. So, just about anyone who wants to enter the program should be "given a chance." Yes, "we are educators," but there are limits to our powers. It took me a while to realize that my magic wand never did work very well. If teacher education program faculty and administrators continue to admit PTs who lack self-confidence, desire to succeed, or knowledge about and openness to difference and diversity, then they have a professional and ethical responsibility to establish opportunities and program continuation checks wherein PTs meet these criteria in order to proceed.

In teacher education, we need to see beyond our students to *their* students. Even if many or most of our PTs will not teach in urban schools, or in schools with diverse student populations, they will be bringing their knowledge and beliefs, their biases and fears, to their students. We owe middle- and upper-middle-class white students a more varied, inclusive, and open-minded education than the one many of us (middle-class whites) received.

Haberman (1996), for example, has long argued for the active recruitment and selection for admission of PTs with favorable dispositions toward difference and diversity, including more people of color. His position is based on evidence that PTs entering teacher education programs with "little or no sensitivity to diversity or with prejudicial attitudes— qualities that are antithetical to culturally responsive teaching—are not apt to change those views within the scope of preservice teacher education" (Villegas & Lucas, 2002, p. xvi). Elsewhere (Haberman, 1995, cited in Ladson-Billings, 1999a, p. 233) has urged recruiting "adults" into urban education programs such as his in Milwaukee. Their admissions interview process is:

> designed to test prospective teachers' persistence, willingness to protect learners and learning, ability to put ideas into action, attitudes toward at-risk students, professional-personal approach to students, understanding of their own fallibility, emotional and physical stamina, organizational ability, and disposition toward cultivating student effort versus innate ability. (Ladson-Billings, 1999a, p. 233)

It is incumbent on those who favor a more open-door policy on admission to teacher education to demonstrate that their program does change not only beliefs but also, and more importantly, the classroom practices of those they eventually recommend for teacher certification. More self-reportedly positive views of difference and diversity following a single course are not sufficient. As has been shown (see Chapter 1), single course effects usually are overwhelmed or washed out by other courses and field experiences; rarely are they shown to positively affect classroom practice. More coherent teacher education programs, however, may accomplish what single courses have not.

Retire the Old Teacher Education Debates and Consider Contemporary Questions

Participating in one or another debate may be enjoyable, but it is most often less influential than shaping the debate in the first place. Just as the way one defines a problem sets the solution path, how a debate is shaped or defined sets the parameters for acceptable participation. I first realized this in the early 1990s, when the public and professional education debates about multiculturalism and more inclusive history curricula were defined by conservative pundits as issues of *pluralism versus unity*. This polarization indicated that a nation, for example, could not embrace both. One was supposed to take sides. It was not a constructive debate. It faded after a while, as other issues gained prominence, but it may reappear in the same or similar form once again.

Similarly, the old debates about more subject matter versus more pedagogy or college/university versus school-based teacher education are more destructive than helpful and ought to be retired. Why not have both, complementary and in relation to each other, working together toward preparing teachers to more constructively engage student difference and diversity?

The old, polarizing debates also serve to pretty much maintain the status quo in teacher education by deflecting attention from, for example, questions of racism and culturally responsive teaching. The old debates might support modest changes akin to the special features in textbooks that do not alter the main story, but they do not admit the substantial changes needed by urban schools and students.

Another contemporary issue involves when-where-how to address the questions of teacher-student difference and diversity that have framed this volume. This should certainly be done in preservice teacher education, and even earlier, as has been emphasized here. I would not, however, support increasing the requirements for initial teacher certification. Even with the best of intentions, loading more requirements on the "front end" of teacher education prior to initial certification and teaching is not likely to be very helpful for constructively engaging student difference and diversity. More hours, course credits, and exams may appear to increase standards and rigor (and enhance the reputations of those supporting them), but they miss the crucial factors of PTs' mindsets and of practice on the ground, with students in schools.

Many, if not most, of the PTs with whom I have worked for more than 30 years are somewhat apprehensive about student-teaching but eager to get out there and see if they can do it, that is, survive as classroom teacher. Too many are impatient with coursework unless they see it as practical—an elusive quality that I have come to see as largely in the eye of the beholder, like beauty. They tend to equate practical with tangible or recipe-like. Their priority is survival, if not success. They do not want to be bothered with complexity or reflection. This mind-set is consistent with long-standing U.S. cultural traditions that value "hands-on" learning, learning on the job, and learning by (not from) experience, even among middle-class and "good" students. As historian Richard Hofstadter (1963) has well documented, anti-intellectualism has been a dominant theme in U.S. history, even in education. Consequently, more front-end requirements for teacher preparation and initial certification are likely to be resisted and resented by PTs, perhaps especially if they call for major changes in PTs' self-concepts, outlooks, and behavior.

The second crucial factor, classroom practice, seems to be a necessary prerequisite to realizing the need for learning and "doing something" to reach diverse groups of students. Perhaps you do have to "be there." Without classroom experience from a teacher's perspective, you do not necessarily recognize the challenges or what it would take to meet them.

For these reasons, I would frame the issue as how (not whether) to advance constructive engagement with student difference and diversity in masters and professional development programs. What might culturally responsive teaching, for example, look and sound like with *my* students in *my* school? How could I get from here to there?

CONCLUDING NOTE

The implications I've drawn raise major challenges for teacher education and raise the bar for teacher educators as well as for prospective and newer teachers. I cannot point to any teacher education programs that incorporate all these recommendations. Unfortunately, such model programs have tended to be short-lived, depending on external funding and/or the energies of visionary, risk-taking faculty members.

Because the ideal 21st-century teacher education program does not now exist does not mean that it is impossible to reach or is not worth pursuing. There is much work to be done. I am hopeful that the teacher education program at my university as well as programs elsewhere will begin or will increase their efforts to assist PTs in engaging student difference and diversity more constructively. If, 10 years from now, constructively engaging student difference and diversity is no longer as difficult for as many new teachers, more students will be completing high school, continuing with postsecondary education, and leading productive, satisfying lives—and many fewer teachers will leave teaching or be described as "burnt out."

Appendix A:
Methodological Note
and Theoretical Perspective

The "project," as I refer to it, was a field study conducted over 1 year at Charter School and 2 at Royalton High School. It involved spending considerable time on-site, sitting in and hanging out, for example, in the office, cafeteria, teachers' workroom, classrooms, and hallways between classes. These experiences and informal conversations were documented as field notes. A key data source consisted of numerous informal conversations with teachers and other school personnel (e.g., head of security, attendance office manager), students, prospective teachers and their university supervisor-mentors. We also conducted and taped semi-structured interviews with the PTs who volunteered to participate, either at the school site or the university. These interview tapes were transcribed for later analysis. Excerpts from the interview transcripts have been edited for clarity without changing the content or meaning. Finally, we collected school and district documents and news reports to provide background.

Although guided by my theoretical perspective and the relevant literature, the analysis of the data collected has been largely inductive, open-ended, and recursive. I did not, for example, fully anticipate the drama of the PTs' initial experience of Royalton High School or the unhelpful power of negative messages about urban schools. I had attended public schools in Chicago (albeit some years ago); my graduating class had fewer than 500 in a high school of 5,000. The region's city schools did not frighten me. Royalton had a good reputation. The university would not knowingly place PTs at a bad or unsafe school. I did not expect the trauma that some PTs experienced at first. Clearly, I needed to de-center myself and go with the flow without sacrificing the project's purposes. Thus, Chapter 2 deals with "getting started" at Royalton.

It is important to recognize and make explicit one's assumptions or theoretical perspective, both to aid readers in understanding where you are "coming from" and to further one's own self-understanding. It is too easy to fool ourselves about our values and priorities when we do not probe our motives, assumptions, and the likely or actual consequences of acting on them. By now, my motives in writing *Diversity and the New Teacher* should be quite clear: to better understand the interaction of individuals and institutional setting during field experience and student-teaching with respect to constructively engaging school and student difference and diversity in order to assist prospective and new teachers in fostering more meaningful student learning and their own success and satisfaction in teaching. By *meaningful learning*, I mean comprehension rather than rote memorization, understanding that is linked to and extends students' prior experiences and knowledge, and critical thinking that involves multiple perspectives. What follows now is a brief account of my theoretical perspective.

My approach to both the project and this book reflects a critical sociology. As in my prior, strongly contextualized work, I draw on C. Wright Mills's history-biography-social structure framework in *The Sociological Imagination* (1959) and Margaret Archer's historical work on education system change as a function of structurally situated and conditioned social interaction (1984). In other words, both individual behavior and social interaction are shaped by the setting or social structure in which they occur, as well as by what people bring with them to the setting (biography), and what has happened in the past influences present options and choices. Here, I also draw from Archer's more recent work on what she calls "the internal conversation" in *Structure, Agency and the Internal Conversation* (2003), which refers to the individual's taking stock of his or her situation and intended project or goal, and then deciding how to proceed. Picture the prospective teacher wanting to succeed, being intimidated by a city school placement, and deciding what to do next. Archer's "internal conversation" can be seen as a theoretical elaboration of the concept of perspective as used by Becker, Geer, Hughes, and Strauss in *Boys in White* (1961), their study of medical students becoming physicians. Their concept of perspective, encompassing one's ideas and actions in a problematic situation, is situated or structurally conditioned, but does not address the interactions among ideas, actions, and situation.

Much earlier, W. I. Thomas and then Willard Waller in *The Sociology of Teaching* (Waller, 1932) described "the definition of the situation" as an "intimately subjective" process

> in which the individual explores the behavior possibilities of a situation, marking out particularly the limitations which the situation imposes upon his behavior [in order to form] an attitude toward the situation, or, more exactly, in the situation . . . group products that we know as folkways, mores

[and norms, standard operating procedures], etc., are . . . elements of the definition of the situation which the individual works out for himself. (pp. 292–293)

Describing one's "definition of the situation" as one of the key sociological constructs for understanding human experience in and around schools, Waller notes that "the school may be viewed as an agency for imposing preformed definitions of situations" (p. 296), primarily on students. However, as Waller also observed, these "preformed definitions" or mores are (re)interpreted by students in pursuit of their interests as they see them. The same can be said of prospective or newer teachers in specific school settings at a particular time.

Waller, Mills, Becker et al. (1961), and Archer can be seen as addressing personal reflection or reflexivity, what Archer calls the reflexive deliberation of social agents. This private cognitive activity that "leads to self-knowledge: about what to do, what to think and what to say" (Archer, 2003, p. 26) both links and mediates structure and agency. The present project emerges from this critically framed interactive tradition to focus on engaging school and student difference and diversity in teacher education and professional development. It is set within a broader critical paradigm that seeks equity and social justice.

Appendix B:
The Prospective Teachers at Royalton and Charter Schools

Royalton, 2004–2005

Amanda	English
Kate	Science
Ken	Science
Malcolm	Social studies
Mark	Social studies
Renee	Social studies

Royalton, 2005–2006

Cora	Science
Ethan	English
Jaclyn	Social studies
Kaitlyn	English
Lynn	Science
Rupert	Social studies

Charter School, 2004–2005

Dante	1st grade
Kirk	5th grade
Sylvia	2nd grade
Tammy	Kindergarten–1st grade

References

Abell, S. K., and Roth, M. (1994). Constructing science teaching in the elementary school: The socialization of a science enthusiast teacher. *Journal of Research on Science Teaching, 31*(1), 77–90.

American Psychological Association. (2003). Guidelines on multicultural education, training, research, practice, and organizational change for psychologists. *American Psychologist, 58,* 377–402.

Archer, M. S. (1984). *Social origins of educational systems.* London: Sage.

Archer, M. S. (2003). *Structure, agency and the internal conversation.* Cambridge: Cambridge University Press.

Becker, H. S., Geer, B., Hughes, E. C., and Strauss, A. (1961). *Boys in white: Student culture in medical school.* Chicago: University of Chicago Press.

Bell, L. A. (2002). Sincere fictions: The pedagogical challenges of preparing white teachers for multicultural classrooms. *Equity & Excellence in Education, 35*(3), 236–244.

Bonilla-Silva, E. (2006). *Racism without racists: Color-blind racism and the persistence of racial inequality in the United States.* (2nd Ed.). Lanham, MD: Rowman & Littlefield.

Brown, E. (2004). What precipitates change in cultural diversity awareness during a multicultural course: The message or the method? *Journal of Teacher Education, 55*(4), 325–240.

Carnegie Forum's Task Force on Teaching as a Profession. (1986). *A nation prepared: Teachers for the 21st century.* New York: Carnegie Forum on Education and the Economy.

Christensen, L. (2001). Where I'm from: Inviting students' lives into the classroom. In B. Bigelow, B. Harvey, S. Karp, and L. Miller (Eds.), *Rethinking our classrooms,* Vol. 2, pp. 6–10. Milwaukee: Rethinking Schools.

Cochran-Smith, M. (1995). Color blindness and basket making are not the answers: Confronting the dilemmas of race, culture, and language diversity in teacher education. *American Educational Research Journal, 32*(3), 493–522.

Cochran-Smith, M., Davis, D., and Fries, K. (2004). Multicultural teacher education: Research, practice, and policy. In J. A. Banks and C.A.M. Banks (Eds.), *Handbook of research on multicultural education,* pp. 931–975. 2nd Ed. San Francisco: Jossey-Bass.

Cornbleth, C. (2003). *Hearing America's youth: Social identities in uncertain times.* New York: Peter Lang.

Davidson, A. L., Yu, H. C., and Phelan, P. (1993). The ebb and flow of ethnicity: Constructing identity in varied school settings. *Educational Foundations*, 7(1), 65–88.

Feagin, J. R., Vera, H., and Batur, P. (2001). *White racism.* (2nd Ed.). New York: Routledge.

Foster, M. (2001). Black teachers on teaching: A collection of oral histories. In B. Bigelow, B. Harvey, S. Karp, and L. Miller (Eds.), *Rethinking our classrooms*, Vol. 2, pp. 181–185.

Gay, G. (2000). *Culturally responsive teaching: Theory, research, and practice.* New York: Teachers College Press.

Gootman, E. (March 17, 2007). The critical years: For teachers, middle school is test of wills. *New York Times*. (www.nytmes.com/2007/03/17/education/17middle.html?ei+5 . . .) Retrieved 3/17/07.

Haberman, M. (1995). *Star teachers of children in poverty.* West Lafayette, IN: Kappa Delta Pi.

Haberman, M. (1996). Selecting and preparing culturally competent teachers for urban schools. In J. Sikula, T. J. Buttery, and E. Guyton (Eds.), *Handbook of research on teacher education*, pp. 747–760. (2nd Ed.). New York: Macmillan.

Hemmings, A. (2003). Fighting for respect in urban high schools. *Teachers College Record*, 105(3), 416–437.

Hofstadter, R. (1963). Anti-intellectualism in American life. New York: Knopf.

Hollins, E. (1995). Revealing the deep meaning of culture in school learning: Framing a new paradigm for teacher preparation. *Action in Teacher Education*, 17(1), 70–79.

Holmes Group. (1986). *Tomorrow's teachers.* East Lansing, MI: The Holmes Group.

Irvine, J. J. (2003). *Educating teachers for diversity: Seeing with a cultural eye.* New York: Teachers College Press.

King, J. (1991). Dysconscious racism: Ideology, identity and the miseducation of teachers. *Journal of Negro Education*, 60, 133–146.

Ladson-Billings, G. (1994). *The dreamkeepers: Successful teachers of African American children.* San Francisco: Jossey-Bass.

Ladson-Billings, G. (1999a). Preparing teachers for diverse student populations: A critical race theory perspective. *Review of Research in Education*, 24, 211–247.

Ladson-Billings, G. (1999b). Preparing teachers for diversity: Historical perspectives, current trends, and future directions. In L. Darling-Hammond and G. Sykes (Eds.), *Teaching as the learning profession: Handbook of policy and practice*, pp. 86–123. San Francisco: Jossey-Bass.

Ladson-Billings, G. (2001). *Crossing over to Canaan: The journey of new teachers in diverse classrooms.* San Francisco: Jossey-Bass.

Lawrence, S. M. (1997). Beyond race awareness: White racial identity and multicultural teaching. *Journal of Teacher Education*, 48(2), 108–117.

Marx, Sherry. (2006). *Revealing the invisible: Confronting passive racism in teacher education.* New York: Routledge.

McIntosh, P. (1992). White privilege and male privilege. In M. L. Andersen and P. H. Collins (Eds.), *Race, class, and gender*, pp. 70–81. Belmont, CA: Wadsworth.

McIntyre, A. (1997). *Making meaning of whiteness: Exploring racial identity with white teachers*. Albany: SUNY Press.

McNeil, L. M. (1986). *Contradictions of control: School structure and school knowledge*. New York: Routledge & Kegan Paul.

Michie, G. (1999). *Holler if you hear me: The education of a teacher and his students*. New York: Teachers College Press.

Michie, G. (2005). *See you when we get there: Teaching for change in urban schools*. New York: Teachers College Press.

Mills, C. W. (1959). *The sociological imagination*. New York: Oxford University Press.

Neville, H., Spanierman, L., and Doan, B. (2006). Exploring the association between color-blind racial ideology and multicultural counseling competencies. *Cultural Diversity and Ethnic Minority Psychology, 12*(2), 275–290.

Nieto, S. (2003). *What keeps teachers going?* New York: Teachers College Press.

Payne, R. K. (1998). *A framework for understanding poverty*. Baytown, TX: RFT.

Pollock, M. (2004). *Colormute: Race talk dilemmas in an American school*. Princeton: Princeton University Press.

Popkewitz, T. S., Tabachnick, B. R., and Wehlage, G. (1982). *The myth of educational reform*. Madison: University of Wisconsin Press.

Rothenberg, P. (1988). Integrating the study of race, gender, and class: Some preliminary observations. *Feminist Teacher, 1988, 3*(3), 37–42.

Schempp, P. G., Sparkes, A. C., and Templin, T. J. (1993). The micropolitics of teacher induction. *American Educational Research Journal, 30*(3), 447–472.

Schofield, J. W. (1982). *Black and white in school: Trust tension or tolerance?* New York: Praeger.

Schofield, J. W. (2001). The colorblind perspective in school: Causes and consequences. In J. A. Banks and C.A.M. Banks (Eds.), *Multicultural education: Issues and perspectives*, pp. 247–267. (4th Ed.). New York: Wiley.

Sleeter, C. E. (1988). Preservice coursework and field experiences in multicultural education: Impact on teacher behavior. Kenosha, WI: University of Wisconsin-Parkside, School of Education. [Cited in Zeichner and Hoeft, 1996]

Sleeter, C. E. (1993). How white teachers construct race. In C. McCarthy and W. Crichlow (Eds.), *Race, identity and representation in education*, pp. 157–171. New York: Routledge.

Sleeter, C. E. (2001). Preparing teachers for culturally diverse schools: Research and the overwhelming presence of whiteness. *Journal of Teacher Education, 52*(2), 94–106.

Sleeter, C. E. (2005). *Un-standardizing curriculum*. New York: Teachers College Press.

Stevenson, R. B. (1990). Engagement and cognitive challenge in thoughtful social studies classes: A study of student perspectives. *Journal of Curriculum Studies, 22*(4), 329–341.

Tatum, B. D. (1997). *"Why are all the black kids sitting together in the cafeteria?" and other conversations about race*. New York: BasicBooks.

Tatum, B. D. (2007). *Can we talk about race? and other conversations in an era of school resegregation*. Boston: Beacon Press.

Tharp, R. (1989). Psychocultural variables and constraints: Effects on teaching and learning in school. *American Psychologist, 44*, 349–359.

Thompson, A. (1999). Colortalk: Whiteness and *Off white*. *Educational Studies*, *30*(2), 141–160.

Villegas, A. M., and Lucas, T. (2002). *Educating culturally responsive teachers*. Albany: SUNY Press.

Waller, W. (1932). *The sociology of teaching*. New York: John Wiley & Sons.

Weiner, L. (2006). *Urban teaching, The essentials*. (Rev. Ed.). New York: Teachers College Press.

Wellman, D. T. (1993). *Portraits of white racism*. (2nd Ed.). Cambridge: Cambridge University Press.

Wideen, M., Mayer-Smith, J., and Moon, B. (1998). A critical analysis of the research on learning to teach: Making the case for an ecological perspective on inquiry. *Review of Educational Research*, 68(2), 130–178.

Zeichner, K. M. (1992). *Educating teachers for cultural diversity*. East Lansing, MI: Michigan State University, National Center for Research on Teacher Learning Special Report.

Zeichner, K. M., and Gore, J. (1990). Teacher socialization. In W. R. Houston, M. Haberman, and J. Sikula (Eds.), *Handbook of research on teacher education*, pp. 329–428. New York: Macmillan.

Zeichner, K. M., and Hoeft, K. (1996). Teacher socialization for cultural diversity. In J. Sikula, T. J. Buttery, and E. Guyton (Eds.), *Handbook of research on teacher education*, pp. 525–547. (2nd Ed.). New York: Macmillan.

Index

About the Author

Catherine Cornbleth is professor of education at the Graduate School of Education, University at Buffalo, State University of New York (SUNY), where she teaches graduate courses in social studies education, curriculum, and critical interpretations of research. She was the founding director of the Buffalo Research Institute on Education for Teaching (BRIET), and continues to work with prospective and newer as well as experienced teachers. She has authored or coauthored several books: *Curriculum in Context* (1990), *The Great Speckled Bird: Education Politics and Multicultural Policymaking* (1995, with Dexter Waugh), and *Hearing America's Youth: Social Identities in Uncertain Times* (2003). She has edited two books: *An Invitation to Research in Social Education* (1986) and *Curriculum Politics, Policy, Practice: Cases in Comparative Context* (2000). Her scholarly articles have been published in journals such as *American Educational Research Journal, Educational Researcher, Journal of Curriculum Studies, Teachers College Record*, and *Theory and Research in Social Education*. Her 1994 *AERJ* article, "Teachers in Teacher Education" (with Jeanne Ellsworth) won the 1995 American Association of Colleges of Teacher Education (AACTE) Outstanding Writing Award. A graduate of the Chicago Public Schools, she taught high school social studies in Texas and Connecticut before returning to graduate school.